Discovering Shakespeare

The Taming of the Shrew

A WORKBOOK FOR STUDENTS

"For those interested in introducing Shakespeare to younger students,

these workbooks should provide valuable assistance. ...

The material is effectively arranged...This workbook might prevent a young student

from giving up on Shakespeare. Instead, that student may fulfill the authors' hope

and "discover the joys of Shakespeare...and move on to

Shakespeare's complete versions with enthusiasm and ease."

—KLIATT

YOUNG ACTORS SERIES

Great Scenes and Monologues for Children

New Plays from A.C.T.'s Young Conservatory Vol. I

New Plays from A.C.T.'s Young Conservatory Vol. II

Great Scenes for Young Actors from the Stage

Great Monologues for Young Actors

Multicultural Monologues for Young Actors

Multicultural Scenes for Young Actors

Multicultural Plays for Children Grades K–3

Multicultural Plays for Children Grades 4–6

Plays of America from American Folktales for Children

Plays of America from American Folktales for Young Actors

Short Plays for Young Actors

Seattle Children's Theatre: Six Plays for Young Actors

Villaggiatura: Goldoni's Trilogy *Condensed for Young Actors*

Loving to Audition: A Young Actor's Workbook

Movement Stories for Children

An Index of Plays for Young Actors

Discovering Shakespeare: *A Midsummer Night's Dream*, A Workbook for Students

Discovering Shakespeare: *Romeo and Juliet*, A Workbook for Students

Discovering Shakespeare: *The Taming of the Shrew*, A Workbook for Students

The Plays of the Songs of Christmas

If you require prepublication information about upcoming Smith and Kraus books, you may receive our semiannual catalogue, free of charge, by sending your name and address to *Smith and Kraus Catalogue*, P.O. Box 127, One Main Street, Lyme, NH 03768. Or call us at (800) 895-4331, fax (603) 795-4427.

Discovering Shakespeare

The Taming of the Shrew

A WORKBOOK FOR STUDENTS

Written and Edited by Fredi Olster
and Rick Hamilton

Young Actors Series

SK

A Smith and Kraus Book

A Smith and Kraus Book
Published by Smith and Kraus, Inc.
One Main Street, PO Box 127, Lyme, NH 03768

First Edition: October 1996
10 9 8 7 6 5 4 3 2 1

Library of Congress Cataloging-in-Publication Date

Discovering Shakespeare :
The taming of the shrew: a workbook for students and teachers / [edited] by Fredi Olster and Rick Hamilton. —1st ed.
p. cm. —(Young actors series. Discovering shakespeare Series)
Includes bibliographical references (p.   ).
Summary: Presents an abridged version of Shakespeare's Taming of the Shrew, discussing the play's language, characters, plot, and how to stage a school production.
ISBN 1-57525-046-2

1. Shakespeare, William, 1564–1616. Taming of the shrew.
2. Shakespeare, William, 1564–1616—Problems, exercises, etc.
3. Shakespeare, William, 1564–1616—Outlines, syllabi, etc.
4. Shakespeare, William, 1564–1616—Dramatic production.
[1. Shakespeare, William, 1564–1616. Taming of the Shrew. 2. Shakespeare, William, 1564–1616—Dramatic production.
3. Theater—Production and direction. 4. Plays—Production and direction.]
I. Olster, Fredi.
II. Hamilton, Rick.
III. Series: Young actors series. Discovering Shakespeare series.

PR2832.T36   1996
822.3'3—dc20   96-38449
CIP
AC

Contents

"How came these things to pass?"

HOW THESE BOOKS CAME TO BE WRITTEN

I have spent most of my life working as a Shakespearean actress. Yet, when I was growing up and studying Shakespeare in school, I hated it! I came to realize that many of my teachers also hated it. And who can blame any of us, we didn't understand it for the most part.

It wasn't until I started acting in Shakespeare's plays at the Oregon Shakespeare Festival in 1970 that I began to feel differently. There, I met Angus Bowmer, the founder of the festival and director of the first play I was to do there, *The Merchant of Venice,* and Rick Hamilton, a young actor at the festival, who was later to become my husband.

Between them, they taught me to love the language and to appreciate the timelessness of the stories. And now, of course, I'm hooked. I would rather act in a play by Shakespeare than any other playwright.

I've come to realize that my experience with Shakespeare is not unique. And it was my desire to share what I have learned from Angus and Rick and the many other directors and actors I've worked with over the years that inspired me to write this workbook.

The immediate impetus came, though, while I was doing a production of *Christmas Carol* in San Francisco. I was playing Mrs. Fezziwig who is a delightful character but who isn't in a lot of scenes. So I had a great deal of time for other activities.

One of them was to start work on *All's Well That Ends Well,* which I was to be in when *Christmas Carol* closed. *All's Well* was a play that I was totally unfamiliar with. I was sitting in my dressing room with my Shakespeare glossaries, dictionaries, and various copies of the play doing my *homework* when my friend Sarah came in and asked what I was up to.

Sarah was then twelve and was playing Young Belle in our production. She and I were old friends having worked together on two shows in the past. I told Sarah what I was doing, and she asked if she could read *All's Well* with me. I said "sure" and we proceeded to read the Helena/Parolles scene in Act 1 together.

Note that this is a particularly difficult scene, full of double-entendre, sexual innuendo, and very complex language. We read together and looked up all the words we didn't grasp.

Let me say here that I have to do this whenever I work on a Shakespeare play that I don't know well. The words he used are different from the ones we now use. In the four hundred years since he wrote these plays, the English language has changed and some of the words Shakespeare used have gone out of fashion or have evolved in their meanings so that we no longer easily understand them.

But with a little practice and *homework* we quickly realize that the ideas he wrote about remain extremely applicable to us.

I came to understand this even more clearly when, after Sarah and I had finished the scene and had discussed what it meant, Sarah said to me, "I'm going to read this to my friends tomorrow at school, this stuff is great and it's so sexy." Well at that moment I realized once again the absolute brilliance of Shakespeare. He had the power to reach out through those four hundred years that separated him and Sarah and thoroughly excite her interest.

Sarah is now a young lady of fourteen and not only has she continued to be excited by Shakespeare, but she has passed on her interest to her younger sister Julia who is ten.

The question then became, how can we (by this time Rick agreed to work on this project with me) make Shakespeare accessible to kids who don't have an actor to sit down and read it with? And that's how the idea for this format came about.

Our objective became: tell the story, introduce the characters, and let Shakespeare's ideas come ringing through. The difficulty, of course, is that wonderfully complex language of Shakespeare's. So we decided the best way to introduce Shakespeare to people who were not familiar with him was, as I had done with Sarah, to translate him into the *vernacular*—that is, our equivalent everyday language.

That way, the new student of Shakespeare can begin to understand the story, the characters, and the ideas without the added obstacle of the four hundred year old words.

Once these elements become clearer and the reader starts to discover the beauty of Shakespeare, as Sarah did, it then becomes even more thrilling to go back to the original language, which is, needless to say, so much richer and more poetic than anything we have replaced it with.

Let us point out here that this workbook is only meant as an introduction to Shakespeare. We are actors and not scholars and would not pretend competency in that world.

Our main objective is to instill a love of Shakespeare and to encourage the next generation of young people to attend our theaters with a true desire to see and support and perhaps act in the works of the incomparable master.

It is our sincere hope that the users of these workbooks will discover the joys of Shakespeare sooner than we were able to and will be tempted to move on to Shakespeare's complete versions of the plays with enthusiasm and with ease.

How to use this book

The Discovering Shakespeare edition of *The Taming of the Shrew*, with its abridged version of the play along with the vernacular translation and supportive chapters, is designed for multiple uses.

1. It serves as a workbook to help in the study of Shakespeare's language. By reading scenes aloud, and using the accompanying vernacular translation to facilitate comprehension, the student will find it easier to understand the language and plot of the play thereby making the study of Shakespeare an enjoyable experience.
2. It serves as a launching pad for a *reading* of the play. Students take on the individual parts, doing research into the characters, and then, with scripts in hand, read the play aloud.
3. It serves as an aid in organizing a simple production of the play for classroom performance.

The facilities available and the needs and interests of the class will determine what would be most useful for the students.

We have included information about *performance* because this material is vital for the understanding of Shakespeare. Shakespeare was first and foremost a man of the theater. To understand him, it is necessary to understand the medium he was writing for.

It is our intention that the vernacular version be employed to facilitate understanding of Shakespeare's language and that Shakespeare's own words be used for performance.

Also, please note that the suggested stage directions, acting notes, character interpretations, etc., reflect our personal opinions and should merely be thought of as a starting place. None of this is in stone; Shakespeare is open to interpretation. Be free and creative in your choices and your work. You are the next generation of Shakespeare students, interpreters, audience, and performers—he is now in your hands, serve him well.

*Within the stage directions an asterisk (*) indicates a suggestion to see the chapter on acting techniques, theatrical conventions, and lazzi.*

Bracketed notations ([ ]) that appear throughout the text are interpretive hints that we've included for actors doing either a reading or a production of the play.

"Whence are you?"

SHAKESPEARE'S SOURCES FOR
THE TAMING OF THE SHREW

A newlywed couple are out for a horseback ride. The sun is shining and everything is fine. Suddenly the man's horse stumbles a little. The man looks at the horse and says, "That's once!"

They continue on and after a while the man's horse stumbles again. The man reins in his horse and—in a very clear voice—says, "That's twice."

They ride on a little further and the man's horse stumbles a third time. The man then dismounts, pulls out a pistol, and shoots his horse.

The bride is horrified and says, "Why on earth did you do that, the horse was fine." The man looks at his bride and says, "That's once!"

That old joke is older than you think. Its origins have been traced back to folktales which were in existence long before the time of Shakespeare. Versions of the tale could be found in many countries throughout the world.

The common feature of the various versions is how a man gets control of his marriage. To do this, according to the tales, the man must do something so outrageous and shocking that his wife will not dare to ever question his authority.

Shakespeare used the situations described in these folktales as the basis for almost all the Petruchio and Kate scenes in *The Taming of the Shrew*.

The original versions of these tales reflected the prevailing attitude of male superiority. It is evidence of Shakespeare's genius that he was able to take the *form* of these tales and use them to tell a story with quite another *content!*

In *Shrew,* we see Shakespeare starting with these stories of male domination and using them to relate the story of the creation of a workable union between two unique and somewhat difficult individuals.

This story of Kate and Petruchio, based on the ancient folk tales, is told against a background of Italian comedy known as *commedia dell'arte.* Commedia dell'arte was a style of theater that had begun some two hundred years earlier in Italy and was loosely based on Greek and Roman comedy traditions.

In its beginnings, commedia dell'arte was a kind of street theater. It could be performed anywhere there was available space and an audience to watch. It was a very flexible form of theater. There were rarely *scripts;* instead there were *scenarios.* These were outlines containing brief descriptions of the scenes in the play along with a list of who was to be in the scene and a description of what had to be accomplished in each scene. The rest was up to the actors.

The characters were drawn from a standard list of character types known as *stock* characters. There was the *lover* type, the *wily servant* type, the *dirty-old-man* type, etc. These were stereotypes rather than individuals. An actor usually played the same character for life, sometimes having inherited that character from his or her parent.

Commedia characters were always played broadly—*very* broadly. Anything to make the character funny was thrown in: twitches, stutters, lisps, pidgeon toes, flatulence, drooling, funny voices, funny walks—all were unashamedly used.

For example, the actor playing the lover would at some point be sure to moan, sigh, stammer, walk into walls, trip, make his voice crack, kiss a tree, etc. And the actor playing the servant known as Arlecchino (who Grumio is fashioned after) would usually specialize in acrobatic skills and would throw these in whenever appropriate. And so on with all the other characters.

The actors also developed a rather elaborate repertoire of *bits, gags,* and *stage business* known as *lazzi,* which they would employ to enliven or accent the telling of the story. Each stock character had his or her own bag of lazzi.

An actor playing in the commedia style must not be afraid to go way out on a limb—with saw in hand! But he must do so with total commitment. The playing of commedia is an art form requiring not only daring, but tremendous skill, creativity, and discipline!

Commedia scenarios usually concerned love intrigues. Young people fell in *love at first sight* and used their servants to help them attain their desires. The Bianca/Lucentio story in *Shrew* comes directly from commedia sources.

The Taming of the Shrew then is based on elements of story and style from commedia dell'arte along with elements of the broad outrageous humor of the traditional folk tales. We will see that under Shakespeare's guidance, these rather two-dimensional worlds will combine to yield a story that goes far beyond what either source originally offered.

"What's the pith of all?"

WHAT'S *THE TAMING OF THE SHREW* ALL ABOUT?

The Taming of the Shrew is a domestic comedy centering around Baptista Minola's problems associated with marrying off his two daughters—one of whom is a shrew—and the man who comes along to marry that shrew.

This basic story has been represented in traditional folklore for ages, and various writers have dealt with it over time. What is unique about Shakespeare's telling of the story is the humanity with which he endows Kate and Petruchio, the central characters in the play.

In the standard telling of the *taming* story, a disorderly wife is beaten, frightened, shocked, abused, and sometimes raped to get her to submit to her husband's wishes.

Shakespeare, on the other hand, has Petruchio achieve his *taming* by teaching Kate to view the world in a new light. Petruchio never once strikes Kate—though she does slap him. He certainly doesn't rape her—instead, he delivers a "sermon of continency" to her on their wedding night. And, as we will see, he goes through "painful labors" in his quest to succeed in bringing about a positive change in Kate. Shakespeare's story is not about the squelching of a spirit, but the releasing of one that has long been hidden.

By the end of *The Taming of the Shrew,* we see that Kate and Petruchio are much more than a couple of brawlers or a woman who has been brow-beaten into submission by an overbearing bully. They are a loving pair who have gained insight and knowledge enabling them to go forth and deal with any situation as a team. They have learned how much stronger they can be acting in unison rather than pulling in separate directions. They are truly *a match!*

Shakespeare also investigates the *masking* and *unmasking* of our true selves in *Shrew.*

Disguise (masks) is a traditional element of commedia dell'arte—usually used by the lovers to gain access to their beloved.

In *Shrew,* Shakespeare takes this notion of disguise and extends it. Not only does he have characters use disguise/masks to *conceal* who they are (Tranio, Hortensio, and the Pedant), he also has characters *unmask* to *reveal* who they are.

Kate's transformation causes her to discard the shrewish mask that she has worn since childhood, and she stands revealed as a truly intelligent, self-aware, loving young woman, while Bianca, having dropped her mask, shows herself to be the real shrew.

"If I get your daughter's love, what dowry shall I have with her to wife?"

ELIZABETHAN MARRIAGE CUSTOMS

In spite of Romeo and Juliet's extreme youth when they eloped, they were the exception to the rule. Most Elizabethan men and women waited until they were in their twenties to marry—much as we generally do today.

Unlike now, though, when relatively few couples have prenuptial agreements, Elizabethans wouldn't dream of marrying without first negotiating a contract arranging the financial terms of the marriage.

This contract was drawn up to guarantee that the couple had sufficient funds to set up a household and to insure that the woman would not become a burden on society should she be widowed.

There were two basic elements of the contract: the *dowry* and the *dower*. The dowry represented the total assets that the bride brought with her into the marriage from her family; this could include lands, goods or actual cash. (In *Shrew,* Baptista offers 20,000 crowns when the marriage takes place and half of his lands when he dies as a dowry for Kate.) The dower represented the assets which the groom's family would guarantee to the bride should she become widowed. (In *Shrew,* Gremio offers *all that he has* as a

dower for Bianca to have when he dies if, as he says, "whils't I live, she will be only mine.")

The contract might also include terms for a *jointure,* which was the gift that the groom's family would give the couple when the marriage took place. A yearly *allowance* from the groom's family might also be determined.

These last two elements were generally considerations only when the couple sprang from noble families. In such cases, the young couple usually had no means of making a living; they merely lived off their families' holdings. Nobles rarely had the opportunity to go out and get a job. They were trained for nothing but fighting for their king and living off their lands.

Dower and *dowry* arrangements, though, applied to almost every marriage. The poorest young lady proudly brought some sort of dowry into her marriage, even if it were just a few shillings and the linens that she had embroidered since childhood. And English law *required* dower arrangements to be made—this was the Elizabethan form of life insurance for women.

"But stay . . . what company is this?"

BRIEF DESCRIPTIONS OF THE CHARACTERS IN *THE TAMING OF THE SHREW*

The Taming of the Shrew opens in Padua—an Italian university town—where Baptista Minola, a successful businessman, is facing the trials and tribulations of marrying off his daughters, Kate and Bianca. His neighbor, Gremio, along with another local, Hortensio are both anxious to court Bianca.

Lucentio, son of Vincentio, a wealthy merchant in Pisa, along with his servants, Tranio and Biondello, comes to Padua to study and immediately falls head over heels in love with Bianca.

Shortly thereafter Petruchio and his servant, Grumio, arrive from Verona to visit their friend, Hortensio, and to look for a wife for Petruchio.

These characters, along with Curtis (another servant of Petruchio's), a Tailor (who makes a gown for Kate), a Pedant (who will help complicate the plot), and a Widow (who is in love with Hortensio) comprise the primary cast list for *Shrew.* Let's now take a look at each of these characters and see how they contribute to the play.

KATHERINA

Katherina Minola (also called Katherine and Kate) is the central character in this play. It is her dilemma and the journey she must take to resolve it that Shakespeare is most concerned with.

When we meet Katherina, she is in trouble. We see a person who not only makes everyone around her miserable—but is miserably unhappy herself. She can't seem to fit into the society in which she lives; she is an outcast, a rebel, a misfit!

How was this sad state of affairs arrived at? We are not given any textual background on her childhood, so we must conjecture. Let's suppose that ever since the day her younger sister Bianca was born, Kate has not only been a distant second in her father's affections, but in everyone else's in the community too. Why?

We can safely assume that Kate and Bianca's mother is dead; she most likely died giving birth to Bianca. Kate, being the elder, knew her mother and suffered horribly at her loss. Bianca, the baby, never experienced this pain. She blithely, happily grew up—being pampered and spoiled as any pretty, little blond-haired baby might be.

Bianca soon learned how to smile and coo and get her own way in everything—while the older Kate wept and pouted and could find no comfort for her loss and no doubt came to resent this new baby who was getting all the attention that she so craved.

The stage is now set, and years later we see these two young ladies locked into their patterns. This is sibling rivalry in the first degree, and Kate is always the loser. Kate has gone from being hurt to becoming enraged, and this has only made matters worse. Every tantrum she throws—every barb she hurls—only serves to prove to all onlookers that Bianca is sweeter and nicer.

Bianca has also mastered the art of false flattery, and everyone, except Kate, seems to fall for it hook, line, and sinker. Kate on the other hand is brutally blunt—saying exactly what she thinks without any editing.

Kate believes that the people around her are shallow and self-involved, and she doesn't try to hide these feelings. She is direct, biting, and constantly on the offensive, and no one dares look beyond her hostile exterior to see the truly gifted person underneath. And Kate is gifted. She is not only beautiful, intelligent, possessed of a magnificent spirit, and honest, but she is also courageous. She is willing to defy convention.

Kate refuses to accept the role of the subservient, "good little girl" expected of young women at this time. She stands up and rebels. But in the process,

Kate has worked herself into a corner. Everybody dislikes her and her sharp tongue, and if she continues in this self-destructive pattern, she will be unhappy and alone forever.

To make matters worse, the time has come when her baby sister is being besieged by ardent admirers, and poor Kate's fate seems to be that of a lonely, old maid—unless something radical can come along to change things for her—and that is just what is about to happen in *Shrew.*

Let's track Kate through the play and see how these changes come about. As soon as Kate comes onstage, we learn a lot about her. The men in her world want nothing to do with her. She is way too much for any of these guys to handle. They are scared to death of her. They call her a "fiend of hell" and a "devil" and from their point of view, she is.

Kate's situation has indeed reached a crisis point. Her father has put out the word that no one will be permitted to court Bianca till Kate is married and that anyone who will take Kate off his hands will receive a huge sum of money.

This is embarrassing and humiliating to say the least! And how does Kate react? In Act 2 scene 1, Kate has tied Bianca's hands and is taking all her frustrations out on her. What we see in this brief scene is their opposite natures coming head to head—Bianca's jibe at Kate as her "elder" sister demonstrates her cloaked, coy nastiness, while Kate's insistence that Bianca *tell the truth* shows Kate as an intolerant bully.

Baptista walks in just in time to catch Kate picking on her baby sister. Bianca immediately starts to weep and Kate has lost again. Kate once more experiences the rejection which she is forever forcing people to demonstrate toward her. But of course, Kate is her own worst enemy. She has never learned how to deal with people except by lashing out.

Then along comes Petruchio and in true commedia dell'arte style, he and Kate fall *in love at first sight.* Sparks fly as soon as they set eyes on each other. But Kate would rather have her teeth pulled than admit that—and even if Kate wanted to, she wouldn't know how. Kate has spent her whole life as a smart-mouthed, rebellious contrarian. How could she possibly respond in any other way but as she does—with barbs and jabs and pokes?

But this guy stays right with her, and that's something she has never experienced! Not only that, but he can outtalk her. So much so that when Baptista comes in to see how their courting is going, Petruchio convinces him that he and Kate are in love. By the time Petruchio leaves, Kate finds herself engaged to be married.

Something inside Kate knows that this relationship just might work. The proof of this is that on the appointed day of marriage, Kate is there all dressed up and ready. And when it looks as if Petruchio might not show up—Kate's tears are real! Just when her heart had begun to soften, her hopes have been dashed.

When Petruchio finally does arrive, her worst fears are confirmed. Petruchio makes a mockery of everything; dress code, manners, even the marriage vows. And to top it off, he refuses to stay for the wedding feast. This is humiliating and infuriating. Kate may be a rebel, but her new husband makes her look like "a lamb, a dove." Kate digs in her heels and tells him where to go.

Kate is not aware of it yet, but there is method in Petruchio's madness. But at the moment all Kate can see is that her plans are being disrupted. Every young woman—even Kate—has fantasies about her wedding day, and Petruchio's actions are certainly not fulfilling any of these!

While Petruchio's behavior flies in the face of all conventions, Kate is suddenly finding herself desperately trying to maintain decorum. The wedding scene ends in uproar with Kate literally being carried off kicking and screaming. For the first time in her life, Kate is protesting *for* convention, not rebelling *against* it!

The trip to Petruchio's house is more of the same. We learn from Grumio's description that when Kate's horse stumbled, Petruchio beat Grumio, and it was Kate who came to Grumio's defense. Kate is here shown trying to help people rather then mistreat them.

Once they arrive at Petruchio's, there is more uproar—flying dinnerware, dousings with water, and servants being scolded. Kate is stunned and again finds herself pleading for kindness and civility.

To further confuse things, when Kate and Petruchio retire to the bridal chamber, rather than going to bed with her, Petruchio gives her a lecture on the virtues of sexual abstinence! Kate is totally bewildered.

Kate doesn't know it, but this is all part of Petruchio's plan, and Grumio is in on it, as we see in Act 4 scene 3, when he refuses to bring her any food. Kate is hungry and exhausted—it's now time for Petruchio to begin to try to make her change her ways.

Kate has spent her life being angry at the world. She is closed off, everything is black and white, right and wrong; she is sardonic and compassionless. Petruchio hopes to teach her to *see* the world differently—with less rigidity and with more joy. He is going to try to show her that the world and everyone in it is not

likely to change, but that her point of view of the world can alter thereby making it a much more pleasant and satisfying place to live in. How is this achieved?

Petruchio brings Kate some food and offers it with one condition—that Kate give thanks for it. Kate doesn't know what to make of this—she's never had to say "thank you" to anyone! But she's starving and finally offers her thanks.

Before she can eat the food, Petruchio tempts her with beautiful new clothing, which he promptly sends back. She is lost! Then, in one of the most beautiful speeches in the play, Petruchio tells Kate that it is *she,* not her accoutrements, that is of value.

If this scene is played correctly, it is tender and touching, and Kate begins to see that there may be method in his madness. More importantly, she begins to realize that this guy may actually be in love with her. Then, just as it looks as if progress is being made, Petruchio begins an argument about the time of day and stomps off leaving Kate even more confused.

The next time we see Petruchio and Kate, they are on the road to Padua. Petruchio refers to the glowing object in the sky as the moon, and when Kate contradicts him, he starts another argument. Kate finally agrees to let Petruchio have his way, and when she concedes that it is the moon, Petruchio immediately reverses himself.

It is at this moment of complete confusion and contradiction that Kate *gets it!* She sees that the world will not change—the sun is the sun and the moon is the moon—but one's *perception* of it may alter.

It is difficult to say exactly what goes on in Kate's mind at this moment. It might be a kind of relaxing or opening or maybe a giant "whew!" But whatever occurs, the change in her demeanor is pronounced. She is now playful and teasing. She sees that winning and losing and being right or wrong sometimes just doesn't matter. Accepting the world on its terms, having fun, and, most importantly, loving and being loved is what counts.

She also sees that Petruchio has not been trying to break her spirit, but is merely asking her to join with him and exercise that spirit in a new and joyful way. That is exactly what Kate does in the scene with Vincentio.

Petruchio and Kate encounter an elderly male traveler on the road, and Petruchio greets him as though he were a young woman and suggests that Kate do the same. Kate promptly does so calling the man, "young, budding, virgin." When Petruchio reverses himself and tells Kate that she is mistaken, Kate, without losing a beat, not only apologizes to the gentleman for her "mad-mistaking" but manages to gently poke fun at Petruchio's sun/moon business. All the while, she conveys quite clearly to Petruchio that she understands what he has just helped her to accomplish. When Kate says "everything I look on seemeth green," she is telling Petruchio that she has arrived at a new perspective and that she is seeing things in a new light.

We see too that all the while Kate is being the perfect lady. Kate is now a "gentlewoman," as Petruchio points out. He is tremendously proud of her and she is mighty happy with herself. Kate's basic ideas have not changed, she is merely looking at things in a new light. She has developed a generosity of spirit and is learning how to present her ideas with such finesse that no one can resist her. She also is realizing that for Petruchio to have gone to all the trouble he has for her sake, he must truly be in love with her.

When they arrive in Padua, Kate and Petruchio watch as events unfold and finally are resolved. Petruchio then asks Kate for a kiss. Kate is shy about kissing, and Petruchio takes her reluctance to be an indication that she is ashamed of him. When he starts off toward home, she stops him and tenderly kisses him—their first *real* kiss.

This scene must not be thought of as an obedience test. Petruchio has let down his guard and is asking for Kate's approval—which she gives him with all her heart. The two have finally come together and have formed a true partnership.

The final scene reveals their partnership to the world. They are now confident of each other's love and can do anything together with ease. When Petruchio asks Kate to demonstrate her *new* self, she does so with glee. She is more than happy to tell her sister and the widow what she thinks of them and yet do so in such a way that makes them look foolish and herself appear the perfect lady.

When she returns to Padua, a new and commandingly confident Kate is revealed; one who causes the people who previously shunned her to sit up and take notice. Lucentio speaks for them when he admires Kate's gracious obedience with, "Here's a wonder." And Baptista expresses his great pride in his daughter's transformation when he says, "I will add unto their losses twenty thousand crowns, another dowry to another daughter, for she is changed as she had never been."

Kate's wild, offending spirit has been *tamed,* allowing her joyous, fun-loving nature—so long buried in her—to be released.

When Kate describes a husband as "one who cares for thee, and for thy maintenance commits his body to painful labors," she means this: hasn't Petruchio just proved his love for her by going through some very "painful labors" for her sake?

Kate, who appeared to be in such terrible straits at the beginning of the play, has now grown into a confident, loving, respected young woman. Petruchio's methods have worked, and they are both delighted at the results!

PETRUCHIO

Petruchio's story is basically that of an unconventional man who finds himself an unconventional woman and, using unconventional methods, insures their happiness together.

Petruchio is a man of great energy. He is bright, inventive, confident and possesses a wonderful sense of irony.

He, like Kate, recognizes that the world is full of foolish, self-centered, overly mannered people but, unlike Kate, he has learned to deal with these people with understanding and with a joyous, outrageous, even *loony* sense of humor.

These attributes have earned him the reputation of being an eccentric—but so what! Petruchio couldn't care less what other people think of him. He is a man who is comfortable with himself; he sincerely likes himself and this gives him a great sense of confidence and allows him a tremendous freedom in what he does.

He is not concerned with gaining approval from others, and appearances don't matter a bit to him. His speech on the subject is one of the most beautiful in the play:

> 'tis the mind that makes the body rich;
> And as the sun breaks through the darkest clouds,
> So honor peereth in the meanest habit.
> What, is the jay more precious than the lark
> Because his feathers are more beautiful?
> Or is the adder better than the eel
> Because his painted skin contents the eye?
> Oh no, good Kate; neither art thou the worse
> For this poor furniture and mean array.

This is a man who sees through facades right to the very heart of things. He knows that a pretty face can front for a shallow mind, and he's not about to be trapped by superficialities.

Petruchio is from Verona. He's been around—he's no boy. He has seen and done many things including having been to war. His father has died and he is the sole heir to his estate, which he has "bettered rather than decreased."

He has independence, wealth, and the freedom to do as he chooses. But there is a big hole in his life—he's never found a woman to share it with him. And now, with his father dead and the estate passed on to him, he would like a wife and an heir.

Much has been written about Petruchio's mercenary approach when it comes to women, but note that for all his apparent bravado about wanting a rich wife, he has come all the way to Padua to find one. Surely, if he were simply looking for a woman with wealth, he could have found one in Verona. Perhaps Petruchio is hoping for something more—and he is about to find it in Padua!

Let's take a look at Petruchio's journey through the play and see how the various facets of his character work for him.

The very first thing we learn about Petruchio is that this guy likes to have fun—he views life as a celebration. This is demonstrated as soon as he appears onstage. He and Grumio may be master and servant, but they are also best friends. When they arrive at Hortensio's, Petruchio says to Grumio, "knock." Grumio knows full well what Petruchio means but decides to have some fun, and he starts to clown around with the meaning of the word *knock.* Petruchio is aware that Grumio is *playing,* and he agrees to be the straight man in the scene. Not for one moment are they serious. It is this sense of fun and of *who cares who's right* that Petruchio will later encourage in Kate.

When Hortensio comes on, Petruchio and Grumio keep on playing the game, and Hortensio swallows it hook, line, and sinker and is convinced that they are really fighting. They have established an appearance of one thing while actually just pulling Hortensio's chain. It is this ability of Petruchio's to disguise reality that will later come in very handy in his *taming* of Kate.

When Petruchio tells Hortensio that he's looking for a wife, Hortensio half jokingly mentions the shrewish, yet rich Kate. It is now that we see Petruchio's *bravado* displayed. He goes on about wanting a rich wife and says that he doesn't care what she's like. Yet—note—it is not until Hortensio tells him that she's the daughter of Baptista Minola (a man that Petruchio's father knew well) and that she is "young and beauteous, brought up as best becomes a gentlewoman" that Petruchio insists, "I will not sleep Hortensio, till I see her."

When Petruchio arrives at Baptista's, we get to see his disarming, loony sense of humor in action. He says to Baptista that he has heard of Kate's "beauty" (which he has), "her wit" (perhaps), "her affability and bashful modesty" (Baptista's getting nervous), her "mild behavior"!!! Baptista is thrown totally off-balance. But that's exactly the effect Petruchio can have on people, and this helps him tremendously in achieving his ends.

It is this eccentric sense of humor that allows him to disguise his true intentions when necessary. On the other hand, when called for, he can come *bluntly to the point!* We see this when he says to Baptista, "tell me, if I get your daughter's love, what dowry shall I have with her to wife?" There is no nonsense here—just "give me the facts, Jack!" This combination of plain talk and outrageous humor makes Petruchio a very effective man.

Note that Petruchio has said, "*if* I get your daughter's love." For all his bravado, he's aware that this is not a forgone conclusion. He wants to meet her and he wants to see if she is agreeable; he is not going to marry her sight unseen just because she's got money. It is only after he and Kate have fallen in love at first sight (as they indeed do) that he prevents Kate from talking Baptista out of the marriage.

But first, the financial agreement must be arranged. As we noted, Petruchio has been criticized by modern writers for being mercenary, but in reality, he is simply following the accepted customs of the time. Money issues were always settled before a marriage could take place. This is actually one of the most conventional things that Petruchio does.

Once the dowry has been settled, Baptista reinforces that Kate must agree before anything can be finalized. Petruchio says "no problem" and just then, in comes Hortensio having had a lute broken over his head thanks to Kate. This makes Petruchio even more excited about meeting her—she is obviously not your average gal!

Baptista goes off to get Kate, and while Petruchio is alone, he reveals to the audience how he plans to woo her: he won't let her *get to him* and no matter what she says, he will be positive.

He then hears her coming and, full of confidence, turns to conquer. Lightning strikes! Petruchio is stopped dead in his tracks. He was not prepared for the dark-eyed beautiful thoroughbred who strides into the room. When his breath finally returns, he manages to squeak out, "Good morrow Kate, for that's your name I hear." Thus begins one of the most famous scenes in Shakespeare.

The dialogue ranges from bright and witty to down and dirty—what starts out as a chat, turns into a brawl with Petruchio winning by a nose. Then, very hastily, before his variances with the truth can be discovered, he and Kate become engaged and he is gone.

Petruchio is now in love. He knows he has met his match, but what is he going to do about it? Petruchio is no pale trembling Lucentio—so blinded by love that he can't see the truth of the situation.

Petruchio can see that Kate is out of control and that she must learn that there is no need to constantly fight the world. He also knows that she must be made to accept that she is lovable and that he does indeed love her. Kate is one in a million and to break her spirit would be to destroy her. He doesn't want to dominate or be dominated—he wants a partner to share his life.

It is during his week away, that he concocts a plan which, with Grumio's help, he will put into action. He will attempt to hold the mirror of Kate's own nature up to her. By acting as outrageously, as irrationally, as antisocially as she does, he hopes to show her a reflection of herself, thereby allowing her to see how ultimately self-defeating and isolating such behavior is.

He begins when he returns to Padua for the wedding. Mayhem ensues. Every rule, every convention is snapped, twisted, and scandalized. It is here that we see his ability to *disguise his intentions* in action. There *is* method to this madness. Petruchio can appear to be a swaggering, loud-mouthed braggart, when in reality he is a cool, deliberate tactician.

On the way home, Kate's horse stumbles—did Petruchio trip the horse up? Everybody winds up in the mud: the horses are *beaten,* Grumio is *beaten,* and Kate finds herself desperately trying to *restore* order.

When they arrive at Petruchio's house, more of the same, with Petruchio berating the servants, ranting and raving, throwing their dinner on the floor, rejecting and offending left and right—again exaggeratingly mirroring Kate's own past behavior. Kate finally says to him, "be not so disquiet; the meat was well if *you were so contented.*" Is Kate beginning to see that it is *one's own perspective* that must change?

When there is nothing left to wreck, Petruchio says, "Come, I will bring thee to thy bridal chamber." Once in the bedroom, another surprise! Instead of taking Kate to bed, Petruchio, at the top of his lungs, gives her a lecture on sexual abstinence and proper deportment. She is now totally confused. Petruchio then stomps out of the room and comes to talk to the audience.

We now see the toll that this is taking on Petruchio. He is as bedraggled as she. He says, "Thus have I politically begun by reign and 'tis my hope to end successfully." Once again we see that there is method in his madness. Petruchio knows that he must teach Kate to alter her behavior if she is ever to be happy in her life. He hopes to make her shed her rigid hostility and adopt a more fluid approach to life.

He knows that to accomplish this worthwhile end, he must be unsentimental and clear and that he must employ what may appear to be harsh methods. In the process he knows too that he must make her realize that he is acting out of love and concern for her—"and I intend that all is done in reverend care of her." By this time we are beginning to appreciate his methods and hope with him that he will "end successfully."

When next we see Petruchio, he is offering food to Kate with one condition—that she simply say "thank you." This is not done to make her grovel but merely to teach her the benefits of politeness and civility.

Before she can finish the food, he continues with his tactics of confusion and contradiction. He tempts Kate with a beautiful cap and gown and then proceeds to take them away. Kate is near tears.

Petruchio now reveals something he believes very deeply. When he says, "'tis the mind that makes the body rich...neither art thou the worse for this poor furniture and mean array," he is telling Kate that it is she herself that is precious to him. She is the reason to celebrate, not clothes or dowries, and Kate is beginning to hear him.

Petruchio continues with his strategy. He begins a nonsensical argument about the time of day and then strides off leaving Kate dumbfounded. Again he is mirroring Kate's own contrary behavior.

Their next scene takes place on the road. Petruchio is being more contradictory than ever. He calls the sun the moon, and when Kate tries to correct him, he insists that it be his way. But even in the face of this apparent struggle, we can see Petruchio's philosophy of life in action. He is still having fun when he says, "Now, by my mother's *son,* and that's myself," he is very cleverly punning on the word "sun."

Kate finally gives in, but Petruchio then reverses himself with "nay then you lie, it is the blessed sun." It is at this moment that Kate *gets it!* Petruchio is beginning to see the light at the end of the tunnel.

In the scene with Vincentio, Petruchio tests her, and here, free from the negativity that has always ruled her, we get to see the gracious, witty, charming Kate who has been hidden for too long. Petruchio is pleased beyond words, and he just watches her and beams. It is here for the first time that Petruchio calls her "gentlewoman." This is said with great love and admiration, and the compliment is not lost on Kate. Petruchio now feels that his mission has been accomplished.

After arriving in Padua, he asks Kate for a kiss. When she seems reluctant, Petruchio fears that she does not love him and all has been for naught.

At this moment, we witness the culmination of the Kate/Petruchio story. We see Petruchio's vulnerability—he wants Kate's love. When Kate gives him a kiss that he won't soon forget, she is not only demonstrating that she loves him, but that she understands and appreciates all his efforts on her behalf. With that kiss, they seal their compact of true respect, camaraderie, and undying love. From that moment on they are a *team*—a pair to be reckoned with.

In the final scene we see Petruchio not only defending Kate against all attacks—as when Baptista says, "thou hast the veriest shrew of all"—but also willing to *bet the farm* on his wife. We watch as he happily and proudly gives Kate the opportunity to dazzle the hometown crowd with her new social mastery—which she most adroitly does!

BAPTISTA

Baptista is a very wealthy, successful businessman in Padua. He has raised his two daughters alone—there is never any mention of a Mrs. Minola! He's tried his best but as we see from the start, he's fighting a losing battle with Kate. She is an out-of-control, sharp-tongued shrew. To make matters worse, his youngest daughter, Bianca, is swamped with suitors, begging Baptista for her hand, while Kate can't get a date!

Baptista decides to issue an edict stating that there will be no more courting of Bianca till Kate is married. He offers a tremendous dowry with Kate and is no doubt hoping that one of Bianca's suitors will either take the bait himself or will help to find someone for Kate.

When Petruchio appears and offers himself as a suitor to Kate, we may wonder at Baptista's apparent reluctance when he says, "But for my daughter Katherine, this I know, she is not for you, the more my grief." This is because Petruchio has just spoken of Kate as "fair...virtuous...affable" and "modest," and Baptista, not realizing that Petruchio is putting him on, fears that when Petrucio meets Kate and learns the truth about her, he will quickly change his mind.

Baptista's hesitates signing any contracts with Petruchio because he knows that Kate has a mind of her own, and he doesn't dare presume to make decisions for her. He agrees to give his consent to the marriage only after Petruchio's fast talking persuades him that Kate is willing to go along.

Once Kate is disposed of, we see a very different Baptista. Convinced of Bianca's obedience, he merely says that whoever offers the "greatest dower" can have her. When Tranio (as Lucentio) offers the most money, Baptista agrees that he shall get Bianca but (being a smart businessman) insists that Vincentio, who is still in charge of the family wealth, approve of the deal.

In Act 5 scene 1, when the deception and elopement is revealed, it is only the real Vincentio's assurance that "we will content you" (pay the agreed upon money) that calms Baptista's anger.

In Act 5 scene 2, after Kate's transformation has been revealed, Baptista demonstrates his joy by giving Petruchio another twenty thousand crowns as "another dowry to another daughter." He is a proud and happy poppa!

Baptista on the one hand must appear to be a practical businessman, yet on the other, he is clearly at the mercy of his daughters. Bianca has him wrapped around her little finger and manipulates him, and Kate bullies him and has him cowed. He therefore must be a combination of shrewd, somewhat silly, and scared.

BIANCA

Bianca means white in Italian. The name brings to mind purity, paleness, fairness, calm. This immediately puts Bianca in sharp contrast to Kate who is described as rough, devilish, froward, hot, irksome, brawling—a shrew! But, as we will come to see in this play, appearances can deceive. What you see is not always what you get.

This is not to suggest that Bianca is a little monster—not at all. She is merely the product of a society that expected certain things from its females. The first and foremost attribute of a proper lady was that she be totally subservient and obedient to her menfolk—first to her father and then to whomever she marries.

Women were expected to be malleable and polite: demure and pretty ornaments for their men. It was nice if they had some musical skill and could chat knowledgeably about poetry, but their prime function was to run the household and to breed a son to carry on the family name.

Bianca seems to have bought into this totally—just look at her response when Baptista tells her to go inside, "Sir, to your pleasure humbly I subscribe." Doesn't she *sound* like a charming, obedient young lady? But in the course of the play, we will see her true colors emerge, and they are not as pure and white as she would like us to think.

Bianca is the baby of the family and is duly treated as such. She is Baptista's little angel—blond and compliant and sweet as can be. When we first meet Bianca, she barely speaks. She merely appears, prettily, coyly, basking in the glory of her adoring daddy and two suitors in hot pursuit who are trying to dissuade her father from his decision to keep her incommunicado until Kate is married.

This is just how Bianca likes things—she is the center of everyone's attention and without having to do a thing, she evokes lovesick sighs from Lucentio, paternal pats from Baptista, and passionate pleading from Hortensio and Gremio.

We can safely assume that Bianca is actually thrilled by her father's edict—what young girl would ever want to be married to Gremio or Hortensio? But when in Act 2 scene 1, we see Kate trying to get Bianca to admit that she can't stand these fellows,

Bianca once again exudes her coy, circuitous manner and evades answering—although she does manage to insert a barb about Kate's age in her otherwise polite sounding responses. And the moment Baptista appears, Bianca produces the tears which garner daddy's sympathies.

When we next see Bianca, she is with her tutors, and we see the manipulative side of her nature again emerging. She *calls the shots* with these guys, playing them off against each other and telling them what she chooses to learn and when she chooses to learn it and they obey. She's good!

By Act 4 scene 2 it is clear that she has chosen the disguised Lucentio as her love. He is young and handsome and by know she has learned that he is the son of one of the richest men in Italy. But does Bianca go to Baptista and say, "listen pop, there's this guy...?" No, Bianca chooses to go right along with the plan to deceive her father. Some good little girl!

Having participated in the deception of Baptista and then cooingly asking and receiving his pardon, we now see her in the last scene—a married lady. It is here that her new husband begins to see her true colors.

She has now gotten everything she wished for and from the security of her wifely perch, we see her not only refuse to come when Lucentio calls for her saying she is "busy," but she publicly calls him a "fool" for having bet on her "duty."

Where is that sweet, obedient little Bianca now? Kate may not have had the skills to unmask her baby sister, but she has the satisfaction now of knowing she was right about her.

LUCENTIO

Lucentio is the son of one of the wealthiest merchants in Italy. He is a young man who's left his home town of Pisa to come to study in Padua.

He arrives in town and, in the true commedia fashion, falls head over heels *in love at first sight* with Bianca, the daughter of Baptista Minola. He is a goner! He says, "I burn, I pine, I perish Tranio, if I achieve not this young modest girl"—and Lucentio and Bianca have not even exchanged a word yet!

Lucentio is the quintessential commedia *lover*. Once hit by cupid's arrow, he loses all sense of reason. His love contrasts with Petruchio's in that although both are *victims* of the *love at first sight* syndrome, Petruchio is rational and deliberate in his pursuit of Kate and along the way actually falls in love with the woman herself, while Lucentio seems to be more in love with the idea of love and, as we see at the end of the play, has barely gotten to know Bianca.

Lucentio is quite innocent and naive, and it is Tranio who concocts the subtleties of the plan which get him into Bianca's home. Lucentio, though, quickly gets into the swing of things as he invents the story of *killing a man* to keep Biondello quiet.

Lovesick Lucentio (disguised as the Greek and Latin scholar, Cambio) hooks up with Gremio who presents him to Baptista. The stage is finally set for Lucentio to *meet* his love.

When we next see the lovers, Lucentio and Hortensio almost come to blows over who shall be first in line to teach (court) Bianca. Lucentio, having already revealed his true identity, gets the nod. He pleads his case once more and Bianca very skillfully, with *come-hither-but-not-too-far* tactics, encourages him. He is now flying! Lucentio even dares to begin thinking of eloping.

By Act 4 scene 2, Bianca has obviously been won. When Lucentio tells her that he is reading "The Art to Love," and she responds with, "and may you prove sir, master of your art," their hearts are pounding, their blood is throbbing, they are quivering with love. When Tranio advises them that he's gotten Hortensio out of the picture and Biondello appears with the news that he's located an impostor Vincentio, they are aflutter with anticipation.

But once the plan has proceeded and Tranio has managed to arrange for Baptista to be out of the house, Biondello has to practically *spell it out* for Lucentio that he's finally gotten his wish and is free to elope with his love.

When Lucentio returns with his *wife* and sees Vincentio, he immediately drops all pretense and confesses the truth to him.

He seems confident that both his father and Baptista will go along with the marriage, and the truth of the matter is, the match could not be more appropriate had the fathers arranged it themselves.

All seems to have worked out perfectly for this young lover—until the last scene that is! That's when we realize that in his rush to court and marry Bianca, Lucentio never really got to know her. He is thoroughly unprepared for her refusal to come when he calls for her and for her public humiliation of him with, "the more fool you, for laying on my duty." Who is this sweet, young thing he has married?

Lucentio has gotten what he wanted but, as the old saying goes, "be careful what you wish for—you just may get it!"

TRANIO

Tranio is based on the commedia dell'arte characters known as the *zanni*. These were the *servant* characters. The particular zanni Tranio is closest to is *Brighella*, the cunning servant who loved to add intrigue to the plot and to stir up the action in order to outwit the old Pantalone.

Tranio's job title is that of Lucentio's servant, but Tranio and Lucentio are more that just man and master. Lucentio refers to Tranio as, "my trusty servant well approved in all" and asks for Tranio's perspective on things with "tell me thy mind." This definitely reinforces the idea that Tranio plays more than a mere servant's role in Lucentio's life.

Vincentio later says of Tranio, "I have brought him up ever since he was three years old." Tranio and Lucentio have grown up together—they have played together, traveled together, studied together. Yes, Lucentio is a rich man's son, and Tranio is from the working class; Lucentio is the master, and Tranio must obey him. But within the framework of their prescribed social status, there is a mutual friendship and a strong sense of loyalty between these two.

Tranio is a very clever, trustworthy fellow who takes his responsibilities seriously, but he is definitely no stick in the mud. His first bit of advice to Lucentio is not to waste all his time studying, "No profit grows where is no pleasure ta'en," in other words—make sure we have a good time!

No sooner are these words spoken than Lucentio falls head over heels in love with the first girl he sees! This is perhaps not quite what Tranio had in mind, but he loyally assists his master in his new pursuit, snapping him out of his love-induced stupor and pointing out the obstacles that stand in the way of his *achieving* his love—namely the fact that Bianca will be locked away until a man can be found for Kate.

It's interesting to note Tranio's reaction to Kate—he says, "That wench is stark mad or wonderful froward." *Wonderful* in Shakespeare's time could mean *marvelously,* and *froward* meant *contemptuous of authority* or *rebellious.* Tranio is obviously impressed by Kate's extraordinary gumption and spunk. Women, even high-born ones, were basically in the same boat as servants—they *had* to obey. Tranio realizes that Kate is not your average Elizabethan chick and is quick to admire this gal who is willing to stand up to authority.

Tranio is also a man of action, and he knows his way around. When Lucentio is lost in his reverie, Tranio pulls him back to reality and works out a plan to help his master get the girl.

In the process of planning, he manages to arrange things so that he himself will have to play the part of *Lucentio* in this little drama—a part that he covets. How many servants wouldn't like to step into their master's shoes, wear his clothing, instruct his other servants, and instantly command the respect of everyone he meets?

Tranio is in his element and he is thriving, playing his new part to the hilt. He appropriately *outhuffs* the overblown suitors when he meets up with them and goes on to impress Baptista when he encounters him. He's having a ball—planning, conniving, and deceiving. This is all right up his alley! In addition, it's all for a good cause—he sincerely wishes Lucentio well.

When Tranio (acting as Lucentio) makes his dower offer for Bianca, he gets mightily carried away. When Baptista insists that Vincentio give assurance of the dower, Tranio realizes he'd better come up with a substitute father and devises a plan to find an impostor.

By Kate and Petruchio's wedding day, Tranio is practically a son-in-law, and it is to him who Baptista turns for comfort when Petruchio is late. Again, Tranio plays the part brilliantly.

While the others are at the ceremony, Tranio takes the opportunity to fill Lucentio in on what's happening about the search for a *father*. It is here that Lucentio tells Tranio that he is considering eloping. Tranio is delighted. He now has a *new* challenge—finding an opportunity to allow Lucentio and Bianca to secretly marry!

By Act 4 scene 2, Hortensio has obviously confided to Tranio his discontent with Bianca's apparent interest in her Latin teacher. Tranio acts appropriately outraged and cleverly convinces Hortensio to take himself out of the picture. One down! Now to take care of Baptista. When Biondello arrives with the news that he's spotted a potential *Vincentio,* Tranio sends Lucentio off and sets to work.

Tranio's manipulation of the Pedant is classic. He first convinces the Pedant that his life is in danger, then offers to save him by allowing him to impersonate Vincentio.

When we next see Tranio, he has coached the Pedant to play the part of Vincentio. He contrives to get Baptista over to his house to sign wedding contracts and then adds, "send for your daughter by your servant here"—indicating Cambio. The stage is now set: Hortensio is gone; Baptista will be busy at the contract-signing; and Lucentio has permission to take Bianca out of the house.

All seems to be going perfectly. But then—the fly in the ointment—who ever expected Vincentio to show up! Tranio holds his own as long as he can in the face of this adversity, furiously acting up a storm to keep the disguise going in order to protect Lucentio.

When Lucentio comes on, Tranio can stand it no longer and high-tails it out as fast as he can. He knows that he's in for it! But Tranio was loyal to the end and as we see by his presence at the feast, he's obviously survived and been forgiven.

BIONDELLO

Biondello is the junior member of Lucentio's retinue. He is younger and less experienced than

Tranio—in fact this is probably his first trip away from Pisa. He's full of enthusiasm, but he's new on the job and just learning the ropes.

He's clever and has a good sense of humor, and we notice immediately that there is nothing *servile* about him. When he comes on and sees Lucentio's change of garb, he responds to Lucentio's query "Where have you been?" with "Where have I been? Nay…where are you? Master, has my fellow Tranio stolen your clothes? Or you stolen his?"—obviously not your cowering servant type.

But he is the new kid on the block and neither Lucentio nor Tranio seem to have sufficient faith in him yet to tell him the truth about what's going on. Lucentio instead tells him a tale about killing a man and needing to be in disguise.

Through the course of the play, we see that Biondello not only proves himself trustworthy, but shows that he's got the brains and initiative to become an excellent servant. By Act 4 scene 4, Tranio says to him, "thou'rt a tall fellow"—high praise for this young man. By now he's been let in on the true circumstances of their undertaking, and he fulfills his assignments admirably.

We see this clever young servant in action in the wedding scene. He's been sent to watch for Petruchio, and when he returns with the news that Petruchio is coming, he responds to Baptista's, "When will he be here?" with the rather cheeky but witty, "When he stands where I am and sees you there!"

In the scene when he tries to fill Lucentio in on the elopement arrangements, we get to see Biondello's sense of fun in action. He playfully tugs his master along until the lovesick Lucentio finally catches on to the plan.

Even when Vincentio shows up, Biondello doesn't lose his cool. When Vincentio says, "Have you forgot me?," Biondello's quick-witted response is, "Forgot you. No, sir. I could not forget you, for I never saw you before in all my life!" Once he figures out the hierarchy of power, this young man should go far!

HORTENSIO

Hortensio is probably a *second* son. This means that his older brother has inherited the family business and most of the family money. Hortensio has been left to, more or less, fend for himself.

He's fairly young and not bad looking, and so his solution to his financial woes is to marry a rich wife. He has surveyed the available market and zeroed in on the Minola family as the best source for wives.

He is far too intimidated by Kate to even consider her, but he figures that Bianca is pretty and young, and while she doesn't come with quite the dowry that Kate offers, she is still the daughter of a very wealthy father.

All he has to do now is talk Baptista and Bianca into the match. But the hitch comes when Baptista announces that Kate has to marry first. Hortensio's money is running low and time is of the essence, so Hortensio determines that the quickest way to get Bianca back out into the dating circles is to help find a guy for Kate.

When his old friend Petruchio shows up in town announcing that he's come to Padua looking for a wife, Hortensio is delighted. He starts to bring up Kate's name, but stops himself saying that he couldn't do that to a friend. But Petruchio—with jaded masculine bravado—insists that he's looking for a rich girl and doesn't much care what she's like.

Hortensio tells him about Kate's good and bad qualities, adding "that were my state far worser than it is, I would not wed her for a mine of gold." Petruchio is undaunted. Hortensio then insists that Petruchio present him to Baptista as a schoolmaster so that he can get into the inner sanctum and woo his locked-away damsel on the sly—another tricky fellow!

It's interesting to note that while Petruchio has made no mention of requiring financial assistance in his wooing of Kate, it is Hortensio who suggests that Gremio kick in monetary support for the cause. Hortensio definitely has money on the brain.

Hortensio refers to Bianca as "the chosen of Signior Hortensio," but we can plainly see that neither Hortensio nor "Licio" (Hortensio's alias while in disguise) is the chosen of Bianca.

Hortensio definitely gets second-class treatment in the disguised wooer department and quite aptly picks up on the fact that Bianca is far more interested in her Latin and Greek studies than she is in music!

When Hortensio finally brings Lucentio in to witness Bianca's *loose moral character,* he is ready to give up on her. He announces that he will forswear her and marry a wealthy widow—no doubt older and less malleable than he'd hoped Bianca to have been, but still *rich!*

In the last scene we see that while Hortensio may have at last achieved financial security, he will undoubtedly have to pay a heavy price for it!

GREMIO

Gremio is referred to by Shakespeare as a *pantalone.* This is a term taken directly from the commedia dell'arte list of stock characters. The pantalone was the wealthy, old, lecherous merchant who is forever pursuing young women.

When we first encounter old Gremio, he is trying to dissuade Baptista from his decision to keep Bianca unmarried until Kate is wed. He wants the pretty, young Bianca for himself.

When Hortensio suggests that they join forces in finding a husband for Kate in order to free Bianca, Gremio promptly agrees, wishing that the man could quickly be found who "would thoroughly woo her, wed her and bed her, and rid the house of her!" Gremio hasn't got time to waste—he's old and he wants Bianca now!

When we next see him, Gremio has hooked up with Lucentio, who is now disguised as Cambio. The sneaky old fox plans to send Cambio in to "plead" his case of love to the off-limits Bianca.

When Hortensio tells Gremio that he has located a wooer for Kate, Gremio—while doubtful any man would actually want her—agrees to help pay for Petruchio's courtship expenses, "provided that he win her." He is willing to give anything to get Bianca.

When Tranio enters and reveals that he, too, wishes to become a suitor to Bianca, Gremio immediately becomes proprietary and tries to convince Tranio to leave her alone.

Once Kate and Petruchio are betrothed, Gremio immediately turns matters back to his own desires for Bianca. When Baptista says that whoever "can assure my daughter greatest dower shall have my Bianca's love," Gremio starts the bidding. He offers his house with all its contents and his farm with everything on it to be willed to Bianca if only she will be his while he lives. He obviously has no heirs and is willing to give his entire fortune to get possession of this tender young thing.

As Tranio ups the ante, Gremio frantically offers more and more till he finally has to admit, "I have offered all, I have no more, and she can have no more than all I have." Gremio's only hope now is that Vincentio will not give his approval to the deal.

In the wedding scene, Gremio who has attended the ceremony recounts Petruchio's outrageous behavior. Did this horrify him or is he delighted to see Kate *out-shrewed* after all the abuse she has offered in her time?

In Act 5 scene 1, Gremio is standing outside Lucentio's house. He is anxiously awaiting the results of the business meeting within. Remember that unless the terms of the dower are assured, Bianca will be his.

But once the real Vincentio arrives and identities are revealed, Gremio acknowledges that his hopes are dashed, and he resignedly follows the others in to share in the feast.

GRUMIO

Grumio is fashioned after the commedia dell'arte servant characters called *zanni*. Grumio is most closely associated with the zanni called *Arlecchino* or *Harlequin*. He's a wiry, fiery little guy who's always looking for action.

Grumio is Petruchio's servant but, more importantly, he functions as Petruchio's number one sidekick and pal. Whatever Petruchio puts out, Grumio is ready to back up.

In their first scene, we get to see their special relationship in action. When Petruchio says "knock," Grumio starts a *riff* on the word, Petruchio picks up on it and the two of them keep going until they exhaust the subject—all the while, thoroughly enjoying each other.

Grumio is like a jazz musician; he can improvise on any theme that happens to catch his fancy. He's a fast-talking, fast-thinking, impish fellow—zany, playful, and blessed with an innate good humor. Even when he returns home, worn out, cold, and bedraggled, he never loses his sense of fun.

It is in his scene with Curtis that we see how much Grumio loves to talk. While Grumio pretends to be upset about Curtis' interruptions, he wouldn't have missed the chance to tell this tale for anything.

Another thing about Grumio is that he loves to *play dumb*. In the scene with Kate when she is begging for food, Grumio pretends to be the innocent with her, working things around till he can finally get her with, "Why then, the mustard without the beef!"

It is in the tailor scene that Grumio's playful, slightly risqué humor comes out. When Petruchio tells the tailor to take the gown "up unto thy master's use," Grumio can't wait to pounce on the opening Petruchio has left and point out the buried sexual reference in this line which serves to mortify the poor tailor.

Grumio may have been born in the lower classes, but he's definitely *top drawer*. He's the kind of guy you'd want in your corner, and Petruchio knows he's lucky to have him. And by the end of the play, we sense that Grumio and Kate will soon be great friends too.

CURTIS

Curtis is second in command in Petruchio's household under Grumio. He's been back home holding down the fort while Petruchio and Grumio have been on the road. When we meet him, Curtis is anxious for news of their new mistress who is about to arrive.

Curtis is a good-natured, sincere, hard-working fellow, but he's no match for Grumio's quick wit and current foul temper. He makes the mistake of interrupting Grumio, and if it were not for Grumio's love of talking, Curtis might have missed out on the tale. But Curtis is no fool and having heard the report of the trip back home, he very aptly concludes that Petruchio "is more shrew than she."

VINCENTIO

Vincentio is one of the richest men in Italy. Baptista calls him "a mighty man of Pisa," and the Pedant refers to him as "a merchant of incomparable wealth."

When we meet him, he is on his way to Padua to visit his son Lucentio. He's a good-natured fellow as we can tell by his reaction to the strange routine that Kate and Petruchio greet him with.

But when they arrive in Padua and Vincentio is confronted with an impostor who claims to be *him* and his own servants deny they know him, he loses it! It is not until he sees that his son is well that he finally regains his composure. Then, aside from wanting revenge on Tranio, he becomes his gracious self again, assuring Baptista that he will "content" him regarding Bianca's dower.

PEDANT

The Pedant is referred to as such because when Biondello first tells Tranio about him, he says he has spotted "a mercatante or a pedant." *Mercatante* means merchant in Italian, and a *pedant* is a schoolmaster.

We never actually discover which of these our Pedant is, but it doesn't matter. What does matter is that this gentleman appears to be *old* enough to be Lucentio's father, *sucker* enough to fall for Tranio's tale, and *scared* enough by it to go along with Tranio's deception of Baptista.

When he meets Baptista, he plays his part sufficiently well to convince Baptista that he's the real thing. And later in Act 5 scene 1, he has obviously become so giddy with his success (or more accurately, with the many toasts that must have been drunk to celebrate the marriage agreement) that he becomes downright cheeky with the real Vincentio when he comes visiting, calling him a "liar" and ordering his arrest and even referring to him as "mad ass." This Pedant has definitely gotten carried away with his part!

TAILOR

This was a time when fashion was very important. Men and women did not go about in casual attire; they dressed up, way up. A wealthy man's outfit could weigh as much as forty pounds, and women's clothing was equally elaborate. The concept of "clothes making the man" was never adhered to more fervently.

In the *tailor scene,* the Tailor tells Petruchio that the gown he has brought is made "just as my master had direction: Grumio gave order how it should be done." Grumio then says, "I gave him no order; I gave him the stuff." Grumio is again playing with words—this time with the word *order.* He is saying that he did not "order" anybody around, he merely gave the dressmaker the "stuff" (the fabrics) and placed an "order" for a gown.

We learn from this exchange that the Tailor is in the employ of a *master.* Clothes-making was a big and profitable business.

Note, too, that members of the fashion industry then, as now, were often stereotyped as eccentric, overdressed dandies, and Shakespeare certainly had these attributes in mind when he created the tailor.

WIDOW

We hear about the Widow long before we meet her. When Hortensio forswears Bianca, he says that he will be "married to a wealthy widow, ere three days pass, which hath long loved" him.

Widows were in a unique position in Elizabethan society. They usually had much more freedom than women in any other category. They were no longer under the control of their fathers, having been married, and when their husbands died they, in effect, became their own *masters*—a very rare situation for a female.

This widow is also *wealthy.* So she is pretty much in a position to call the shots, which she certainly looks to be doing with Hortensio in the final scene. She is no shrinking violet; she has Hortensio cowering and is not the least bit shy about speaking her mind to Petruchio. Who's the shrew?

SERVANT

The servant at Baptista's house is one of many in the household. He or she might be young and wary or old and jaded—your choice.

The Taming of the Shrew

CAST LIST

BAPTISTA MINOLA, a rich man of Padua	Bap
KATHERINA (also called Katherine and Kate), eldest daughter of Baptista	K
BIANCA, youngest daughter of Baptista	Bi
GREMIO, rich old man of Padua, suitor to Bianca	Gre
HORTENSIO, another suitor to Bianca	Hor
LUCENTIO, young man from Pisa, suitor to Bianca	Luc
TRANIO, servant to Lucentio	Tra
BIONDELLO, another servant to Lucentio	Bio
PETRUCHIO, gentleman of Verona, suitor to Kate	Pet
GRUMIO, servant to Petruchio	Gru
CURTIS, another servant to Petruchio	Cur
TAILOR, dressmaker to Kate	Tailor
PEDANT, an old man from Mantua	Ped
VINCENTIO, Lucentio's father	Vin
WIDOW, loves Hortensio	Wid
SERVANT, works for Baptista	Servant

Listed on the right are abbreviations of the characters' names. These abbreviations are used in the stage directions, which give blocking suggestions for a production of the play.

Act One • Scene 1   scene description

In Act 1 scene 1 of *Shrew,* we are in the town square of Padua where we meet Lucentio and his servant, Tranio. They have just arrived, and we learn that Lucentio has come to Padua to study philosophy. Tranio advises his master not to neglect his social life while pursuing his intellectual studies. Lucentio is anxious to get settled, but they must wait for Biondello, another servant, before they can get going.

While they are waiting, Baptista enters with his two daughters, Katherina and Bianca, along with Bianca's suitors, Gremio and Hortensio. Baptista is telling the suitors that he has made up his mind not to allow Bianca to marry until a husband is found for Katherina. He says that if either Gremio or Hortensio is interested in Kate, they are welcome to court her. They both quickly shy away from that suggestion. Kate assures them that they have nothing to fear, implying that she would never have anything to do with them anyway.

Tranio, who has been watching all this with Lucentio, is impressed by Kate's spunkiness. Lucentio only has eyes for fair Bianca.

Baptista, trying to get Bianca away from her suitors, tells her to go inside the house, and she says she will pass her time alone reading and practicing her music. (Lucentio is falling under her spell.)

Baptista tells the suitors that he is seeking teachers for Bianca's music and poetry education, and then he goes into the house encouraging Kate to remain outside, which Kate refuses to do. (Note that if he had encouraged her to *come in*—she would no doubt have refused to do that!)

Gremio and Hortensio, disappointed that they will no longer have the opportunity to court Bianca, decide they will try to locate teachers for her.

Hortensio points out that in order to free Bianca from her father's decree, they must join forces and find a man willing to marry Kate. Gremio believes this is an impossibility, but Hortensio tries to convince him that there must be men in the world who would marry her if they were offered enough money. They agree to begin their search, and they depart from the square.

Tranio and Lucentio step out from their hiding place, and we realize that Lucentio has fallen head over heels in love with Bianca. Tranio points out that Baptista's ruling will prevent Lucentio from

Act One • Scene 1   vernacular

[enter Lucentio and Tranio]

LUCENTIO:

Tranio, because of my great desire to
see beautiful Padua, center of the arts,
I have arrived—armed with my father's
good will and your good company. My trusty
servant, well accomplished in everything,
let us here begin a course of learning
and intellectual study. Therefore Tranio,
for now I will study virtue and philosophy.
Tell me what you think.

TRANIO:

Kind master, I agree with everything you say;
I'm glad you still wish to study philosophy,
but good master, don't let us become
sticks in the mud, I beg you—
"all work and no play makes Jack a dull boy!"

LUCENTIO:

Thank you, Tranio, your advice is good.
If Biondello were here, we could
get settled. But look; who's this?

*[enter Baptista, Katherina, Bianca,
Gremio and Hortensio]*

BAPTISTA:

Gentlemen, stop pestering me,
for I have definitely decided not to
let my younger daughter marry, before
I have found a husband for the elder.
If either of you love Katherina,
you have my permission to court her.

GREMIO:

She's too rough for me. There,
there Hortensio, will you marry her?

HORTENSIO:

No! *[to Katherina]* Unless you were made
of gentler, milder stuff.

KATHERINA:

Truly sir, you have nothing to worry about!

Act One • Scene 1 **original abridged**	Act One • Scene 1 **stage directions**

[enter Lucentio and Tranio]

LUCENTIO:
Tranio, since for the great desire I have
to see fair Padua, nursery of arts,
I am arrived, armed with my father's
good will and thy good company.
My trusty servant, well approved in all,
here let us institute a course
of learning and ingenious studies.
Therefore, Tranio, for the time I study
virtue and philosophy. Tell me thy mind.

*(ladder is set UR [see prop notes];
"Town Square" sign visible;
Luc & Tra enter DR, speaking;
Tra stops DRC, Luc X C, looking around)*

(Luc X DC)

TRANIO:
Gentle master, I am in all affected as yourself;
glad that you continue your resolve,
to suck the sweets of sweet philosophy,
only, good master, let's be no stoics I pray—
"no profit grows where is no pleasure ta'en."

(X to Luc)

LUCENTIO:
Gramercies, Tranio, well dost thou advise.
If Biondello wert come, we could
put us in readiness. But stay; what
company is this?

(ad libs from offstage DL; Luc & Tra hide
behind ladder;* Luc on R side of ladder,
peeking around from sides to listen)*

*[enter Baptista, Katherina, Bianca,
Gremio and Hortensio]*

BAPTISTA:
Gentlemen, importune me no farther,
for I firmly am resolved not to
bestow my youngest daughter,
before I have a husband for the elder.
If either of you love Katherina,
leave shall you have to court her.

*(Bap enters DL; Gre & Hor follow;
end with Bap C, Gre DL of him,
Hor DR of him, K & Bi DL, K
R of Bi)*

(Bi coyly waves to audience)
(K turns to audience & sneers)

GREMIO:
She's too rough for me. There, there,
Hortensio, will you any wife?

HORTENSIO:
No! *[to Katherina]* Unless you were
of gentler, milder mold.

(Hor X DS to be on level with K)

KATHERINA:
In faith sir, you shall never need to fear!

*(on "in faith," K X to Hor pointing at
his chest; when he looks down, K flicks
his nose, after lazzi,* she says rest of line,
then X to L of Bi, laughing)*

Act One • Scene 1 scene description

Cont.

courting Bianca. Lucentio remembers that Baptista was seeking schoolmasters for Bianca. He and Tranio hit on a plan that will allow Lucentio to pretend to be a teacher so that he can get in to see Bianca. Tranio meanwhile will pretend to be Lucentio and fulfill his duties as the wealthy Vincentio's son in Padua.

Biondello turns up at this point and Lucentio—obviously not trusting Biondello with the real story—tells him that Tranio is impersonating him in order to save his life and that Biondello must go along with the ruse. Lucentio further complicates the plot by telling Tranio that—disguised as *Lucentio*—he should offer himself to Baptista as a suitor to Bianca.

Act One • Scene 1 vernacular

HORTENSIO:
Lord, save us from devils like her!

GREMIO:
And me too, good Lord!

TRANIO: *[impressed]*
Master! That gal is either stark mad, or wonderfully disobedient.

LUCENTIO:
But in the other I see mild behavior and sobriety.

BAPTISTA:
Bianca, go in. *[Bianca sighs]*
And don't be unhappy, good Bianca.

KATHERINA: *[disgusted at Bianca's phony act]*
Spoiled brat!

BIANCA:
Sister, don't be nasty. *[to Baptista]* Sir, to follow your wishes is my humble desire: I shall remain alone with my books and instruments and will read and practice all by myself.

LUCENTIO:
Tranio! It's as though a goddess were speaking.

GREMIO:
Why will you lock her up, Signior Baptista, instead of this devil? *[indicating Kate]*

BAPTISTA:
Gentlemen, I've made up my mind. Go in Bianca. *[she exits]* And, since she takes great delight in music, instruments and poetry, I will keep schoolmasters in my house, capable of teaching her. If either you, Hortensio, or Signior Gremio, you, know of any, send them to me. And so farewell. Katherina, you may stay. *[he exits]*

Act One • Scene 1 **original abridged**	Act One • Scene 1 **stage directions**

HORTENSIO:
From all such devils, good Lord, deliver us!

(Xing back to Bap, making the sign of the cross)

GREMIO:
And me too, good Lord!

(makes the sign of the cross)

TRANIO: *[impressed]*
Master! That wench is stark mad,
or wonderful froward.

(aside* to Luc DS of ladder)

LUCENTIO:
But in the other do I see mild behavior
and sobriety.

(aside to Tra DS of ladder)

BAPTISTA:
Bianca, get you in. *[Bianca sighs]*
And let it not displease thee, good Bianca.

KATHERINA: *[disgusted at Bianca's phony act]*
A pretty pet!

(says this to audience pointing at Bi)

BIANCA:
Sister, content you. *[to Baptista]* Sir,
to your pleasure humbly I subscribe: my
books and instruments shall be my company,
on them to look and practise by myself.

(Bi X to L of Bap; Gre counters* L, "drooling" over Bi)

LUCENTIO:
Tranio! Thou mayest hear Minerva speak.

(aside to Tra as before)

GREMIO:
Why will you mew her up, Signior Baptista,
for this fiend of hell? *[indicating Kate]*

(K takes step to Gre & growls; he moves close to Bi for protection)

BAPTISTA:
Gentlemen, I am resolved. Go in Bianca.
[she exits] And, for I know she taketh
most delight in music, instruments and
poetry, schoolmasters will I keep within
my house, fit to instruct her. If you,
Hortensio, or Signior Gremio, you, know
any such, prefer them hither. And so
farewell. Katherina, you may stay. *[he exits]*

(Bap takes Bi arm, escorts her UC, she exits; Bap turns DS to finish speech)

(exits UC)

Act One · Scene 1   vernacular

KATHERINA:
And I trust I may go too. What, shall
I be told what to do! Ha! *[she exits]*

GREMIO:
You can go to the devil! No one here will
stop you. Hortensio, this is one helluva
mess. But since I love Bianca, if I can, in
any way, find an appropriate teacher for
her, I will send him to her father.

HORTENSIO:
So will I, Signior Gremio. But a word,
I beg you. It's in our best interest,
to make one thing come to pass.

GREMIO:
What's that, I ask?

HORTENSIO:
Indeed sir, to get a husband for her
sister.

GREMIO:
A husband! A devil.

HORTENSIO:
I say, a husband.

GREMIO:
I say a devil! Do you think, Hortensio,
even though her father is very rich, that
any man would be such a fool to be
married to that devil?

HORTENSIO:
Tush, Gremio! Though she's too much for
you or me to take, why man, there are
men alive who would take her with all
her faults—and enough money.

GREMIO:
I'm not so sure.

Act One • Scene 1 original abridged	**Act One • Scene 1 stage directions**

KATHERINA:
And I trust I may go too. What, shall I be appointed hours! Ha! *[she exits]*

(Xing between Gre & Hor, she pushes them apart, exits UC)

GREMIO:
You may go to the devil! Here's none will hold you. Hortensio, our cake's dough on both sides. Yet, for the love I bear my sweet Bianca, if I can by any means light on a fit man to teach her, I will wish him to her father.

(recovering, shaking his fist toward UC then X to Hor)

HORTENSIO:
So will I, Signior Gremio. But a word, I pray. It toucheth us both, to labour and effect one thing specially.

GREMIO:
What's that, I pray?

HORTENSIO:
Marry sir, to get a husband for her sister.

GREMIO:
A husband! A devil.

HORTENSIO:
I say, a husband.

GREMIO:
I say, a devil! Think'st thou, Hortensio, though her father be very rich, any man is so very a fool to be married to hell?

HORTENSIO:
Tush, Gremio! Though it pass your patience and mine to endure her, why man, there be good fellows in the world would take her with all faults—and money enough.

GREMIO:
I cannot tell.

Act One•Scene 1   **vernacular**

HORTENSIO:
Truly. But, by helping Baptista's oldest
daughter to find a husband, we will set
his youngest free to get a husband. What
do you say, Signior Gremio?

GREMIO:
I agree! And I wish I had someone here
in Padua to begin the wooing, who would
thoroughly woo her, wed her and bed her,
and rid the house of her! Come on. *[they
exit]*

TRANIO: *[coming out of hiding]*
I beg, sir, tell me, is it possible that
love has so suddenly snared you?

LUCENTIO:
Oh Tranio, till it just happened, I never
believed it could. But look! Tranio,
I'll burn, I'll pine, I'll perish, Tranio,
if I don't get this girl. Advise me, Tranio
—I know you can; help me, Tranio—I know
you will.

TRANIO:
Master, you looked so longingly at the
maid, perhaps you missed the meat of the
matter.

LUCENTIO:
Oh yes, I saw sweet beauty in her face.

TRANIO:
Didn't you see anything else? Did you
get a load of her sister!

LUCENTIO:
Her blessedness and sweetness was all I saw.

TRANIO: *[aside]*
Well then, it's time to wake him from
his trance. *[to Lucentio]* Come on, awake
sir! If you're in love with the maiden,
better make a plan to win her. This is
the deal: her older sister is so nasty and biting,

HORTENSIO:
'Faith. But come, by helping Baptista's
eldest daughter to a husband, we set his
youngest free for a husband. How say you,
Signior Gremio?

GREMIO:
I am agreed! And would I had him in
Padua to begin his wooing, that would
thoroughly woo her, wed her and bed her,
and rid the house of her! Come on. *[they
exit]*

TRANIO: *[coming out of hiding]*
I pray sir, tell me, is it possible that
love should of a sudden take such hold?

LUCENTIO:
Oh Tranio, till I found it to be true,
I never thought it possible. But see!
Tranio, I burn, I pine, I perish, Tranio,
if I achieve not this young modest girl.
Counsel me, Tranio, for I know thou canst;
assist me Tranio, for I know thou wilt.

TRANIO:
Master, you looked so longly on the maid,
perhaps you marked not what's the pith
of all.

LUCENTIO:
Oh yes, I saw sweet beauty in her face.

TRANIO:
Saw you no more? Marked you not her sister!

LUCENTIO:
Sacred and sweet was all I saw in her.

TRANIO: *[aside]*
Nay then, 'tis time to stir him from
his trance. *[to Lucentio]* I pray, awake
sir! If you love the maid, bend thoughts
and wits to achieve her. Thus it stands:
her elder sister is so curst and shrewd,

(getting very excited)

(they exit SR)

*(Luc starts to X DS of ladder
to UC in a trance; as Luc X
in front of Tra, Tra steers
him D to C)*

(quivering with love)

(heads UC toward Bi again)

*(Tra gets him and steers him
D to C once more)*

(Luc Xing UC again)

*(X to Luc, brings him D to C,
claps hands loudly to "awaken"
him)*

that until her father gets her married off,
master, your love has to live virginally at home.

LUCENTIO:
Ah! What a cruel father. But didn't you
note that he made a point of trying to
get schoolmasters to teach her?

TRANIO:
Yes, by God, I did sir—and now I've
got it! You will be a schoolmaster and
become her teacher—that's the plan!

LUCENTIO:
It is. Can I do it?

TRANIO:
Not possible. For then, who would be you
and do what you need to do here in Padua
as Vincentio's son?

LUCENTIO:
Don't worry, I see it all now! We haven't
been seen by anyone, nor does anyone know
who's the servant and who's the master
—then it makes sense that—you'll be
the master, Tranio, in my place! I will
be someone else; someone from Florence,
or a man from Pisa. Tranio, take my hat
and coat—when Biondello arrives, he
shall wait on you, but I will instruct
him first so that he doesn't blab.

TRANIO:
Briefly sir, since this is what you want,
I am happy to become Lucentio, because
I love Lucentio.

LUCENTIO:
Tranio, do it, because Lucentio's in love.
[seeing Biondello] Here comes the rascal.
Boy, where have you been?

BIONDELLO: *[enters]*
Where have I been? Why, what's this, where
are you? Master, has my pal Tranio stolen

that till the father rid his hands of her,
master, your love must live a maid at home.

LUCENTIO:
Ah! What a cruel father. But art thou
not advised he took some care to get her
schoolmasters to instruct her?

TRANIO:
Ay, marry, am I sir—and now 'tis plotted!
You will be schoolmaster and undertake the
teaching of the maid—that's your device!

LUCENTIO:
It is. May it be done?

TRANIO:
Not possible. For who shall bear your
part and be in Padua here, Vincentio's
son?

LUCENTIO:
Content thee, for I have it full! We
have not yet been seen in any house, nor
can we be distinguished by our faces for
man or master—then it follows thus—
thou shalt be master, Tranio, in my stead!
I will some other be; some Florentine, or
man of Pisa. Tranio, take my hat and cloak   *(they exchange hats & coat)*
—when Biondello comes, he waits on thee,
but I will charm him first to keep his
tongue.

TRANIO:
In brief sir, sith it your pleasure is,
I am content to be Lucentio, because so
well I love Lucentio.

LUCENTIO:
Tranio, be so, because Lucentio loves.
[seeing Biondello] Here comes the rogue.
Sirrah, where have you been?   *(calling off DR)*

BIONDELLO: *[enters]*   *(enters DR, X between Luc &*
Where have I been? Nay, how now, where are   *Tra, looking back & forth*
you? Master, has my fellow Tranio stolen   *between them, confused & amused)*

your clothes? Or did you steal his?
Come on, what's going on?

LUCENTIO:
Boy, this is no time to joke. In order
to save my life, your pal Tranio here
has put on my clothes and is pretending
to be me. Because since I came ashore,
I killed a man in a fight and I fear it
was witnessed. Pretend to be his servant.
You understand me?

BIONDELLO:
Yes sir! Not one bit.

LUCENTIO:
And don't even utter the name "Tranio"—
Tranio is changed into Lucentio. Let's
go! *[to Tranio]* There's one other thing
you have to do; make yourself one of these
wooers. If you want to know why, just
know I have my reasons. *[they exit]*

    Now we meet Petruchio and his servant
Grumio who have just arrived in Padua from
Verona. They are in front of Hortensio's house and
are having a *misunderstanding* about Petruchio's
use of the word "knock."
    Petruchio has told Grumio to "knock me here
soundly"—meaning that Grumio should knock at
Hortensio's door. Grumio is interpreting this to
mean that his master has commanded him to *beat
him up.* (Is this really a misunderstanding or is
Grumio just messing with Petruchio?) Just as they
are about to get into it, Hortensio appears and
ends the fray.
    Petruchio tells Hortensio that Antonio,
Petruchio's father, has died and that he has come
to Padua to find a wife. Hortensio begins to tell his
friend about Kate but stops himself saying that
Petruchio is too good a friend to introduce him to
such a shrew even if she is very rich. Petruchio says

[enter Petruchio and Grumio]
PETRUCHIO:
To Verona, I've said good-by for a while,
to see my friends in Padua. And of all
of them, my best friend is Hortensio,
and I know, this is his house. Here, my
man Grumio, knock I say.

GRUMIO:
Knock sir! Who should I knock? Is there
any man who has *defamed* your dignity?

PETRUCHIO:
Villain, I say knock me here soundly.

GRUMIO:
Knock *you* here sir? Why sir, what am I
sir, that I should knock you here sir?

your clothes? Or you stolen his?
Pray, what's the news?

LUCENTIO:
Sirrah, 'tis no time to jest. Your fellow
Tranio here, to save my life, puts my
apparel and my countenance on.
For in a quarrel, since I came ashore,
I killed a man and fear I was descried.
Wait you on him as becomes.
You understand me?

BIONDELLO:
I sir! Ne'er a whit.

LUCENTIO:
And not a jot of Tranio in your mouth—
Tranio is changed into Lucentio. Let's
go! *[to Tranio]* One thing more rests that
thyself execute; to make one among these
wooers. If thou ask me why, sufficeth my
reasons are both good and weighty. *[they exit]*

*(Luc & Tra each grab one of
Bio arms & bring him D to
edge of stage)*

*(taking Tra DL as he speaks,
Bio following)*

(they exit DL)

[enter Petruchio and Grumio]
PETRUCHIO:
Verona, for a while I take my leave,
to see my friends in Padua. But, of all,
my best beloved friend, Hortensio, and I
trow this is his house. Here, sirrah
Grumio, knock I say.

GRUMIO:
Knock sir! Whom should I knock? Is there
any man has rebused your worship?

PETRUCHIO:
Villain, I say knock me here soundly.

GRUMIO:
Knock *you* here, sir? Why sir, what am I
sir, that I should knock you here sir?

*(Pet enters UL, Gru behind;
as Pet X DC, Gru X to ladder,
brings it to US of SR entrance,
reveals "Hor House" sign, tosses
sheet offstage; after Pet says
"I trow," Gru whistles—Pet turns,
sees "Hor House" & X to RC)*

*(shadow-boxing around Pet, with
imaginary opponent, pretending
not to understand)*

*(Xing to L of Pet, still playing
dumb)*

. *Cont.*

he doesn't care how shrewish she is as long as she is wealthy.

Hortensio fills Petruchio in about Katherina. He then suggests that Petruchio, who is anxious to meet Kate, take him along disguised as a music teacher and offer him to Baptista as an instructor for Bianca. He is hoping that he may, so disguised, have the opportunity to court her while pretending to teach her.

Gremio now appears with Lucentio, who is disguised as *Cambio*, a Greek and Latin scholar. Hortensio, Petruchio, and Grumio stand aside and listen to their conversation.

Obviously Lucentio/Cambio has convinced Gremio that he can teach Bianca poetry, and we pick up their conversation with Gremio instructing Cambio to teach Bianca about "love" and to plead his case for him. Cambio agrees to this—but we know better!

Hortensio greets Gremio, and they tell each other about their respective plans for Bianca's education. Just as an argument is about to start about who is the more deserving suitor, Hortensio tells Gremio about Petruchio and his willingness to court Katherina.

Gremio seems somewhat skeptical that anyone would undertake this, but Petruchio convinces him that he is serious. Hortensio then talks Gremio into helping pay for Petruchio's courtship expenses.

At this point Tranio, who is disguised as Lucentio, enters along with Biondello. He asks the assembled gentlemen how to get to Baptista's house and proceeds to declare himself a suitor to Bianca. This naturally upsets Gremio and Hortensio but Tranio/Lucentio persists. Petruchio explains the requirement that Baptista has set forth about finding a husband for Katherina before anyone can court Bianca. Tranio agrees to chip in for Petruchio's courtship expenses, and they all depart.

PETRUCHIO: *[threateningly]*
You rascal, I tell you to knock me at this gate, and rap me well, or I'll knock you straight.

GRUMIO: *[aside]*
My master is testy! *[to Petruchio]* If I should knock you first, I know who would come out the worst!

PETRUCHIO:
Will you not do it? If you won't knock, I'll wring it!

GRUMIO:
Help masters, help! My master's crazy.

PETRUCHIO:
Now knock, when I tell you, villain!

HORTENSIO: *[entering]*
Hold on! What's the matter? My old friend Grumio! And my good friend Petruchio!– What are you doing in Verona?

PETRUCHIO:
Signior Hortensio, are you here to break this up?

HORTENSIO:
Get up Grumio, get up—we will settle this quarrel.

GRUMIO:
If this isn't a good reason for me to quit this job—listen sir, he told me to knock him and rap him soundly, sir. Well, is that any way for a servant to treat his master?

PETRUCHIO:
A boneheaded rascal! Good Hortensio, I told the idiot to knock on your gate, and couldn't get him to do it—for love nor money.

Act One • Scene 2 **original abridged**	Act One • Scene 2 **stage directions**

PETRUCHIO: *[threateningly]*
Villain, I say knock me at this gate, and rap me well, or I'll knock your knave's pate.

GRUMIO: *[aside]*
My master is grown quarrelsome! *[to Petruchio]* I should knock you first and then I know after who comes by the worst.

(turns to audience, then back to Pet)

PETRUCHIO:
Will it not be? An you'll not knock, I'll ring it!

(backing Gru up SR)

GRUMIO:
Help, masters, help! My master is mad.

(Gru ducks up & around ladder, appearing again DL of ladder)

PETRUCHIO:
Now knock, when I bid you, sirrah, villain!

HORTENSIO: *[entering]*
How now? What's the matter? My old friend Grumio! And my good friend Petruchio!—How do you all at Verona?

(Pet catches him in a headlock, throws him toward SR & X DC just as Hor enters SR; Hor catches Gru, then sees Pet, lets go of Gru; Gru lands on floor; Hor X to Pet, embraces him)

PETRUCHIO:
Signior Hortensio, come you to part the fray?

HORTENSIO:
Rise Grumio, rise—we will compound this quarrel.

(Xing to Gru, helping him up)

GRUMIO:
If this be not a lawful cause for me to leave his service—look you sir, he bid me knock him and rap him soundly, sir. Well, was it fit for a servant to use his master so?

(playing the wounded victim)

PETRUCHIO:
A senseless villain! Good Hortensio, I bade the rascal knock upon your gate, and could not get him for my heart to do it.

Act One • Scene 2   **vernacular**

GRUMIO:
Knock at the gate! Oh *puh-leez!* Did you not plainly say—"My man, knock me here, rap me here, knock me well and knock me soundly?"—And now you come up with knocking at the gate?

PETRUCHIO:
Squirt, get lost or shut up, I warn you.

HORTENSIO:
Petruchio, patience! This is an unfortunate occurrence between him and you —your trusty, pleasant servant, Grumio! Now tell me, dear friend, what happy gale blows you to Padua?

PETRUCHIO:
The same wind that scatters young men over the world to seek their fortunes. Signior Hortensio, this is how it is: my father, Antonio, is deceased, and I have thrust myself into the world to find a wife and thrive as best I can. I've got money in my pocket and more at home and so have come abroad to see the world.

HORTENSIO:
Petruchio, shall I speak frankly with you and introduce you to a nasty, ill-tempered wife?—And yet I promise you she is rich—very rich—but you're too good of a friend for me to wish you to her.

PETRUCHIO:
Signior Hortensio, between friends like us, few words are needed—so, if you know one rich enough to be Petruchio's wife, even if she's stinky, old, nasty, and mean or even worse, I don't care! I'm here to wive it wealthily in Padua; if wealthily, then happily in Padua.

HORTENSIO:
Petruchio, since we've gone this far,

Act One·Scene 2   original abridged | **Act One·Scene 2   stage directions**

GRUMIO:
Knock at the gate! Oh heavens! Spake
you not these words plain,—"Sirrah,
knock me here, rap me here, knock me well,
and knock me soundly?"—And come you
now with knocking at the gate?

(shadow-boxing)

PETRUCHIO:
Sirrah be gone, or talk not, I advise you.

(pretended threat, starts toward Gru)

HORTENSIO:
Petruchio, patience! This is a heavy
chance 'twixt him and you—your trusty,
pleasant servant, Grumio! Tell me now,
sweet friend, what happy gale blows you
to Padua?

(stopping Pet & taking him DC)

PETRUCHIO:
Such wind as scatters young men through
the world to seek their fortunes. Signior
Hortensio, thus it stands with me:
Antonio, my father, is deceased, and
I have thrust myself into this maze, to
wive and thrive as best I may. Crowns
in my purse I have and goods at home, and
so am come abroad to see the world.

HORTENSIO:
Petruchio, shall I then come roundly to
thee and wish thee to a shrewd ill—
favored wife? And yet I'll promise thee
she shall be rich—very rich—but thou
art too much my friend, and I'll not wish
thee to her.

PETRUCHIO:
Signior Hortensio, 'twixt such friends
as we, few words suffice—therefore, if
thou know one rich enough to be Petruchio's
wife, be she foul, old, curst and shrewd
or worse, she moves me not! I come to
wive it wealthily in Padua; if wealthily,
then happily in Padua.

HORTENSIO:
Petruchio, since we are stepped thus far

I'll go on. Petruchio, I can introduce
you to a wife who is wealthy, young and
beautiful, brought up as a young lady
should be. The only thing wrong—and
that's enough—is that she's unbelievably
nasty, abusive and contrary, so much so
that were I in worse shape than I am,
I would not wed her for a mine of gold.

PETRUCHIO:
Hortensio, hush—you don't know the
power of gold! Tell me her father's name
and that's all I need.

HORTENSIO:
Her father is Baptista Minola, a kind
and courteous gentleman; her name is
Katherina Minola, well-known in Padua for
her scolding tongue.

PETRUCHIO:
I know her father, though I don't know
her, and he knew my deceased father well.
Hortensio, I will not sleep till I see her.

HORTENSIO:
Wait Petruchio, I must go with you. Because
Baptista is keeping my treasure locked
up—his youngest daughter, beautiful
Bianca. He has given an order that no
one shall be able to court Bianca, till
Katherine the curst has got a husband.

GRUMIO:
Katherine the curst! Of all titles for
a girl, that title is the worst.

HORTENSIO:
Now shall Petruchio do me a favor; and
offer me, disguised, to old Baptista,
as a schoolmaster, knowledgeable in music,
to instruct Bianca, so that I may, by
this scheme, have the opportunity and
time to court her alone.

in, I will continue. I can, Petruchio,
help thee to a wife with wealth enough,
and young, and beauteous, brought up as
best becomes a gentlewoman. Her only
fault—and that is faults enough—is that
she is intolerable curst, and shrewd, and
froward, so beyond all measure, that were
my state far worser than it is, I would
not wed her for a mine of gold.

PETRUCHIO:
Hortensio, peace—thou know'st not gold's
effect! Tell me her father's name and 'tis
enough.

HORTENSIO:
Her father is Baptista Minola, an affable
and courteous gentleman; her name is
Katherina Minola, renowned in Padua for
her scolding tongue.

PETRUCHIO:
I know her father, though I know not her,
and he knew my deceased father well. I
will not sleep Hortensio, till I see her.

HORTENSIO:
Tarry Petruchio, I must go with thee. For
in Baptista's keep my treasure is—his
youngest daughter, beautiful Bianca. This
order hath Baptista ta'en, that none shall
have access unto Bianca, till Katherine
the curst have got a husband.

GRUMIO:
Katherine the curst! A title for a maid,
of all titles the worst.

HORTENSIO:
Now shall my friend Petruchio do me grace;
and offer me, disguised, to old Baptista
as a schoolmaster, well seen in music, to
instruct Bianca, that so I may, by this
device, have leave and leisure to court
her by herself.

(takes a step toward DR)

(Hor stops him immediately)

(Xing to R of Hor)

GRUMIO: *[aside]*
See—to trick old folks, how
young folks will scheme!
Master, master, look there—who
is that?

HORTENSIO:
Quiet Grumio—it is the rival for my
love. Petruchio, step aside a moment.

GREMIO: *[enter Gremio and Lucentio, now
disguised as Cambio]*
Listen up sir, these are all books about
love, and see that you read nothing else
to her. You understand me?

LUCENTIO:
Whatever I read to her, I'll plead your
case just as though you were there
yourself. Yes, and perhaps more
successfully than you could, unless you
too were a scholar, sir.

GREMIO: *[aside]*
Oh, this learning! What a thing it is!

GRUMIO: *[aside]*
Oh this birdbrain! What an ass he is!

PETRUCHIO:
Shut up, nitwit.

HORTENSIO:
Good day to you, Signior Gremio!

GREMIO:
And good to see you, Signior Hortensio.
Do you know where I am going?—To Baptista
Minola's. I promised to find a schoolmaster
for pretty Bianca, and by good fortune,
I have found this young man; he is well
read in poetry and other things,—all
good, I assure you.

Act One · Scene 2 **original abridged**	Act One · Scene 2 **stage directions**

GRUMIO: *[aside]*
See—to beguile the old folks, how the young folks lay their heads together! Master, master, look about you—who goes there?

(to audience)

(looking off DR)

HORTENSIO:
Peace Grumio—it is the rival of my love. Petruchio, stand by a while.

(whispering*, they all X & "hide" behind ladder)

GREMIO: *[enter Gremio and Lucentio, now disguised as Cambio]*
Hark you, sir, all books of love, and see you read no other lectures to her. You understand me?

(enter DR, Luc carrying books)

(Xing DC as they speak)

LUCENTIO:
Whate'er I read to her, I'll plead for you as firmly as yourself were still in place. Yea, and perhaps with more successful words than you, unless you were a scholar, sir.

GREMIO: *[aside]*
Oh this learning! What a thing it is!

GRUMIO: *[aside]*
Oh this woodcock! What an ass it is!

(still up at ladder)

PETRUCHIO:
Peace, sirrah.

HORTENSIO:
God save you, Signior Gremio!

(X to between Gre & Luc, slight bow* to Gre)

GREMIO:
And you're well met, Signior Hortensio. Trow you whither I am going?—To Baptista Minola. I promised to inquire about a schoolmaster for the fair Bianca, and by good fortune, I have lighted on this young man; well read in poetry and other books,—good ones, I warrant ye.

(slight bow to Hor)

(indicating Luc, Hor "snobbily" dismisses Luc)

HORTENSIO:
That's good. And I have met a gentleman,
who has promised to help me locate a fine
musician to instruct fair Bianca, who
is so beloved by me.

GREMIO:
Beloved by me, and I'll prove it.

HORTENSIO:
Gremio, this is not the time for us to get into it.
Listen to me, here is a gentleman, who I
happened to meet; who will attempt to woo
curst Katherine; yes, and marry her too,
if her dowry's good enough.

GREMIO:
I'll believe it, when I see it. *[privately
to Hortensio]* Hortensio, have you told
him about her faults?

PETRUCHIO:
I know she is an annoying, quarrelsome
harpy; if that's all, masters, I see no problem.

GREMIO:
You don't say, friend? Where are you from?

PETRUCHIO:
I was born in Verona, old Antonio's son.
My father is dead, his whole fortune came
to me, and I hope a good, long life to
see.

GREMIO:
Oh sir, your life, with such a wife would
be strange. But if you're so inclined,
by God, go for it—I'll assist you every
way I can. But, will you woo this wild
cat?

PETRUCHIO:
Will I live? Why else did I come here?
Do you think a little shouting can
intimidate me? In my time, haven't I heard
lions roar? Haven't I heard giant cannons

HORTENSIO:
'tis well. And I have met a gentleman,
hath promised me to help me to another,
a fine musician to instruct fair Bianca,
so beloved of me.

GREMIO:
Beloved of me, and that my deeds shall prove.

(X to Hor so they are nose-to-nose)

HORTENSIO:
Gremio, 'tis now no time to vent our love.
Listen to me, here is a gentleman, whom
by chance I met; will undertake to woo
curst Katherine; yea, and to marry her,
if her dowry please.

(backing off a bit to calm things down, gesturing to Pet who starts Xing DS while Gre & Hor are talking; he ends up between them with his arms on their shoulders)

GREMIO:
So said, so done, is well. *[privately
to Hortensio]* Hortensio, have you told
him all her faults?

(trying to whisper across to Hor)

PETRUCHIO:
I know she is an irksome, brawling scold;
if that be all, masters, I hear no harm.

GREMIO:
No—say'st me so, friend? What countryman?

PETRUCHIO:
Born in Verona, old Antonio's son. My
father dead, my fortune lives for me,
and I do hope good days and long to
see.

GREMIO:
Oh sir, such a life, with such a wife,
were strange. But if you have a stomach,
to't a' God's name—you shall have me
assisting you in all. But will you woo
this wild cat?

PETRUCHIO:
Will I live? Why came I hither, but to
that intent? Think you a little din can
daunt mine ears? Have I not in my time
heard lions roar? Have I not heard great

*(Pet backs Gre to DLC edge
of stage, turns Xing up to
C; Hor & Luc counter to DRC)*

Act One • Scene 2   vernacular

in the battlefield? In the middle of battle,
haven't I heard loud alarms, horses neighing
and trumpets clanging? And you
tell me now about a woman's tongue that
can't be half as loud as the sound of
a chestnut exploding in some farmer's
fire. Tush, tush! You might as well be
afraid of the bogeyman.

GREMIO: *[impressed]*
Hortensio, hear that! This gentleman is
welcome.

HORTENSIO:
I promised we would chip in, and cover
his costs to woo her, whatever they be.

GREMIO:
And so we will, provided that he wed her.

GRUMIO: *[aside]*
I wish I were as sure that I'd get a good dinner.

*[enter Tranio, dressed as Lucentio, and
Biondello]*
TRANIO:
Gentlemen, God bless you! Tell me, I beg
you, which is the best way to get to
Signior Baptista Minola's?

BIONDELLO:
The man that has the two fair daughters?

TRANIO:
Yes, he's the one, Biondello.

GREMIO:
Excuse me sir, you don't mean her to uh...

TRANIO:
Perhaps I do sir, what's it to you?

PETRUCHIO:
Not the quarrelsome one, if you please.

ordnance in the field? Have I not in a
pitched battle heard loud 'larums,
neighing steeds, and trumpets' clang?
And do you tell me of a woman's tongue
that gives not half so great a blow to
hear, as will a chestnut in a farmer's
fire? Tush, tush! Fear boys with bugs.

GREMIO: *[impressed]*
Hortensio, hark! This gentleman is
happily arrived.

HORTENSIO:
I promised we would be contributors,   *(Xing to R of Gre)*
and bear his charge of wooing, whatsoe'er.

GREMIO:
And so we will, provided that he win her.

GRUMIO: *[aside]*
I would I were as sure of a good dinner.

[enter Tranio, dressed as Lucentio, and   *(Tra, followed by Bio enters*
Biondello]   *UL; Tra X C; Bio stops UL of*
TRANIO: *Tra; Pet counters RC)*
Gentlemen, God save you! Tell me, I
beseech you, which is the readiest way
to the house of Signior Baptista Minola?

BIONDELLO:
He that has the two fair daughters?

TRANIO:
Even he, Biondello.

GREMIO:
Hark you sir, you mean not her to...

TRANIO:
Perhaps sir, what have you to do?

PETRUCHIO:
Not her that chides, I pray.

Act One • Scene 2 vernacular

TRANIO:
I don't like quarrelers sir; Biondello,
let's go.

LUCENTIO: *[privately to Tranio]*
Well done, Tranio.

HORTENSIO:
Sir, let me have a word with you; are you a
suitor to the maiden you're talking about,
yes or no?

TRANIO:
And if I were sir, is that an offense?

GREMIO:
No, if without another word, you get
yourself hence.

TRANIO:
Why sir, I ask you, aren't the streets
as free for me as for you?

GREMIO:
But she is not.

TRANIO:
Why's that, I ask you?

GREMIO:
For this reason if you must know, that
she is the chosen love of Signior Gremio.

HORTENSIO:
Because she's the chosen of Signior Hortensio.

TRANIO:
Easy, my masters! If you are gentlemen,
listen to me patiently. Baptista is a
noble gentleman, who's well aware who
my father is; and his daughter might have
more suitors, and I might be one of them.
And I will be.

HORTENSIO:
Sir, let me ask you, have you ever seen
Baptista's daughter?

TRANIO:
I love no chiders sir; Biondello, let's away.

(they start off DR)

LUCENTIO: *[privately to Tranio]*
Well begun, Tranio.

(whispers to Tra as Tra passes him)

HORTENSIO:
Sir, a word ere you go; are you a suitor to the maid you talk of, yea or no?

(Xing to L of DC)

TRANIO:
An if I be sir, is it any offence?

(Xing to R of DC)

GREMIO:
No, if without more words, you will get you hence.

(X DL of Hor)

TRANIO:
Why sir, I pray, are not the streets as free for me as for you?

(steps down to be level with Gre)

GREMIO:
So is not she.

TRANIO:
For what reason, I beseech you?

GREMIO:
For this reason if you'll know, that she is the choice love of Signior Gremio.

HORTENSIO:
That she's the chosen of Signior Hortensio.

(Xing down to be nose-to-nose with Gre)

TRANIO:
Softly, my masters! If you be gentlemen, hear me with patience. Baptista is a noble gentleman, to whom my father is not unknown; and, his daughter may more suitors have, and me for one. And so she shall.

(Gre & Hor turn to listen with Hor standing slightly UR of Gre)

HORTENSIO:
Sir, let me be so bold as ask you, did you yet ever see Baptista's daughter?

Act One · Scene 2   vernacular

TRANIO:
No sir; but I do know that he has two;
one as famous for her scolding tongue
as is the other for her beautiful modesty.

PETRUCHIO:
Sir, the first one's for me; let her alone.

GREMIO:
Yeah, leave that challenge to great Hercules.

PETRUCHIO:
Sir, understand this—the youngest
daughter, whom you're after, her father
keeps out of the reach of suitors, and
will not let her become engaged until
the elder sister's married—the younger
then is free to wed, but not before.

TRANIO:
If that is the case, sir, then our fate is
in your hands.

HORTENSIO:
Sir, what you say is true, and since you
wish to be a suitor, you must come along
with us, show your gratitude to this gentleman,
to whom we're all indebted.

TRANIO:
Sir, I will not be slack. Fellows, let's
go. *[all exit]*

Act Two · Scene 1 scene description

Here we get a glimpse of life at home with Kate and Bianca. It is obviously not peaceful and poor Baptista just doesn't know how to deal with them.

At this moment, the suitors arrive with their disguised teachers. Petruchio offers himself as a suitor to Katherina and presents Hortensio, who is now disguised as *Licio*, to instruct the girls in music.

Act Two · Scene 1   vernacular

[enter Kate and Bianca]
BIANCA:
Good sister, don't humiliate me—untie
my hands! I'll do whatever you tell me
to—I know I must obey my elders.

Act One · Scene 2 original abridged	**Act One · Scene 2 stage directions**

TRANIO:
No sir; but hear I do that he hath two;
the one as famous for a scolding tongue
as is the other for beauteous modesty.

PETRUCHIO:
Sir, the first's for me; let her go by.

(Xing DR of Tra)

GREMIO:
Yea, leave that labour to great Hercules.

(taking one step DS)

PETRUCHIO:
Sir, understand this—the youngest
daughter, whom you hearken for, her
father keeps from all access of suitors,
and will not promise her to any man, until
the elder sister first be wed—the
younger then is free, and not before.

TRANIO:
If it be so, sir, you are the man must
stead us all.

HORTENSIO:
Sir, you say well, and since you do
profess to be a suitor, you must, as we
do, gratify this gentleman, to whom we
all rest generally beholden.

(stepping D to Tra)

TRANIO:
Sir, I shall not be slack. Fellows, let's
begone. *[all exit]*

*(Luc steps US allowing Pet, Tra, Hor, & Gre
to exit DR; Luc & Bio follow; Gru reveals
"Bap House" sign, exits DR)*

Act Two · Scene 1 original abridged	**Act Two · Scene 1 stage directions**

*(Servant enters SL with two stools which
he places on DC edge of stage, as K & Bi
enter SL; Bi hands tied with rope which K
holds, K pulls Bi down & around to DRC; Bi
ends on her knees; Servant escapes off SL)*

[enter Katherina and Bianca]
BIANCA:
Good sister, wrong me not—unbind my
hands! What you will command me will I
do—so well I know my duty to my elders.

Act Two · Scene 1 scene description

Cont.

Baptista is reluctant to believe that Petruchio is actually willing to court Katherina.

Gremio, anxious not to be left out, steps forward to present his scholar. Baptista, noting the newcomer Tranio, asks him what he wants. Tranio tells him that he wishes to add his name to Bianca's list of suitors and offers some Latin and Greek books and a lute as his contribution to the girls' education.

Baptista sends Cambio and Licio off to meet their pupils. Petruchio, impatient to get on with the financial arrangements of the courtship, asks Baptista about the amount of the dowry that he is willing to offer with Katherina. Baptista offers half of his lands when he dies and upon the day of marriage twenty thousand crowns. This is obviously an impressive amount. Petruchio tells Baptista that if Kate should become widowed, she will be amply taken care of.

Petruchio suggests they draw up the necessary papers, but Baptista hesitates saying that Petruchio will first have to obtain Katherina's love. Petruchio tells Baptista not to worry about that minor detail—he is confident.

Hortensio/Licio reappears having obviously run into some trouble. He explains to the others that Kate took offense at his instruction and hit him over the head with the lute. This description delights Petruchio. Baptista sends Licio off to work with Bianca and tells Petruchio he will send Kate to meet with him.

While Petruchio is waiting, he tells the audience his plan: he will take no offense at anything that Kate says to him and will pretend that he is charmed by her sweet nature.

She appears and he greets her calling her *Kate*, just as Baptista had done. Kate, obviously ready to take offense at anything, tells Petruchio that her name is *Katherina*. Petruchio stands right up to her and says she is known as *Kate*. Furthermore, he is aware of her reputation as "Kate the curst," but that he still finds her extremely attractive. He then proceeds to tell her that he knows her to be mild, virtuous, and beautiful and that he has come to woo her to be his wife.

This sets them off on a series of exchanges that allows them to size each other up. The result is that

Act Two · Scene 1   vernacular

KATE:

Of all your suitors, I order you to tell
whom you love the best; see you don't lie.

BIANCA:

Believe me sister, I haven't yet seen
that special someone whom I could love
more than anyone else.

KATE:

You spoilt brat—you're lying! *[she strikes her]*

BAPTISTA: *[entering]*

Why, what's this? Poor girl, she weeps.
[to Kate] Go, leave her alone. Aren't
you ashamed. Why do you hurt her? When
did she ever say a word against you?

KATE:

She insults me with silence and I'll be
revenged. *[she goes for Bianca]*

BAPTISTA:

What, right in front of me? Bianca go inside.
[she exits]

KATE:

What! Now I see—she's your favorite.
Don't talk to me, I will go sit and weep—
till I can find the moment for revenge.
[she exits]

BAPTISTA: *[aside]*

Was ever a gentleman so distressed as I?
But who's here?

*[enter Gremio with Lucentio (as Cambio),
Petruchio with Hortensio (as Licio), Tranio
with Biondello who carries a lute and
books]*

GREMIO:

Good morning, neighbor Baptista.

BAPTISTA:

Good morning, neighbor Gremio; *[to others]*
God bless you, gentlemen.

KATE:
Of all thy suitors here I charge, tell
whom thou lov'st best—see thou dissemble
not.

BIANCA:
Believe me sister, I never yet beheld that
special face which I could fancy more than
any other.

KATE:
Minion, thou liest! *[she strikes her]*

(hits floor DS of Bi with rope;
Bi rises, tries to run away, they
end L of ladder as Bap enters
SL Xing between them; Bi weeps,
Bap unties her hands, keeps
rope, comforts Bi)

BAPTISTA: *[entering]*
Why how now? Poor girl, she weeps. *[to
Kate]* Go, meddle not with her. For shame!
Why dost thou wrong her? When did she
cross thee with a bitter word?

KATE:
Her silence flouts me and I'll be revenged!
[she goes for Bianca]

(lunges for Bi; Bap grabs K,
holds her while K tries to
break loose)

BAPTISTA:
What, in my sight? Bianca get thee in.
[she exits]

(Bi exits SL)

KATE:
What! Now I see—she is your treasure.
Talk not to me, I will go sit and weep—
till I can find occasion for revenge.
[she exits]

(finally breaking loose)

(K exits SL)

BAPTISTA: *[aside]*
Was ever gentleman thus grieved as I?
But who comes here?

(straightens himself up, puts
rope in belt or pocket, ends
C, knocking* from DR)

*[enter Gremio with Lucentio (as Cambio),
Petruchio with Hortensio (as Licio),
Tranio with Biondello who carries a lute
and books]*

(enter DR in a line Xing to
R of Bap; Gre first, then
Luc, Pet, Hor [disguised]
Tra, Bio [with lute & books])

GREMIO:
Good morrow, neighbor Baptista.

BAPTISTA:
Good morrow, neighbor Gremio; *[to others]*
God save you, gentlemen.

Act Two · Scene 1 scene description

Cont.

Petruchio is now more committed than ever to make Kate his wife.

When Baptista, Gremio, and Tranio reenter, Petruchio tells them that all is arranged. When Kate objects, Petruchio explains that this is part of their plan and that Kate will still appear to be curst when they are with other people.

He goes on to say that they will be married on Sunday and that he must depart to purchase the necessary rings and clothing for the wedding. Kate and Petruchio exit in opposite directions, while the stunned onlookers stand and watch.

Now that Kate is engaged, Gremio and Tranio/Lucentio proceed to vie for Bianca's hand in marriage. Baptista tells them that whoever can offer the greatest financial settlement will have Bianca. Tranio/Lucentio outbids Gremio, and Baptista tells him that if he can get his *father* to guarantee the offer, Bianca shall be his wife, if not, she will marry Gremio. Baptista and Gremio leave, and Tranio sets off to find someone to act the part of Lucentio's father to make the guarantee.

Act Two · Scene 1 vernacular

PETRUCHIO:
And you too, good sir; let me ask you, have you got a pretty and virtuous daughter called Katherina?

BAPTISTA:
I have a daughter sir, called Katherina.

PETRUCHIO:
I am a gentleman from Verona sir, who having heard of her beauty and wit, her affability and bashful modesty, her wonderful qualities and mild behavior, boldly offer myself as a guest, so I might see for myself, all that I have heard.
And I would like to present you with a man, skilled in music, to instruct her.
His name is Licio.

BAPTISTA:
You're welcome sir; and he too for your sake. But as for my daughter Katherine, I am sure, she is not for you, the more's my grief.

PETRUCHIO:
I see that you do not intend to part with her; or else you don't like me.

BAPTISTA:
Don't misunderstand me, I merely am saying what I believe. Where are you from sir? What is your name?

PETRUCHIO:
Petruchio is my name; Antonio's son.

BAPTISTA:
I know him will. You are welcome for his sake.

GREMIO:
Let us get a word in too. Down boy! You're very pushy.

PETRUCHIO:
Oh pardon me, Signior Gremio.

PETRUCHIO:
And you good sir; pray, have you not a daughter called Katherina, fair and virtuous?

(X DS of Gre & Luc to Bap; Gre & Luc counter R)

BAPTISTA:
I have a daughter sir, called Katherina.

PETRUCHIO:
I am a gentleman of Verona sir, that hearing of her beauty and her wit, her affability and bashful modesty, her wondrous qualities and mild behavior, am bold to show myself a guest within your house to witness that report which I so oft have heard. And I present you with a man of mine, cunning in music to instruct her. His name is Licio.

(indicating Hor who X between Bap & Pet, bowing to Bap)

BAPTISTA:
You're welcome sir; and he for your sake. But for my daughter Katherine, this I know, she is not for you, the more my grief.

(guides Hor around so he ends L of Bap, turns back to Pet)

PETRUCHIO:
I see you do not mean to part with her; or else you like not of my company.

BAPTISTA:
Mistake me not, I speak but as I find. Whence are you sir? What may I call your name?

PETRUCHIO:
Petruchio is my name; Antonio's son.

BAPTISTA:
I know him well. You are welcome for his sake.

GREMIO:
Let us speak too. Bacare! You are marvellous forward.

(pulling Luc, Gre pushes Pet US & X to R of Bap; Pet counter to R of Luc)

PETRUCHIO:
Oh pardon me, Signior Gremio.

Act Two · Scene 1   vernacular

GREMIO:
Neighbor, to show my affection,
I offer you this young scholar, who is
as clever in Greek, Latin and other
languages as the other is in music. His
name is Cambio.

BAPTISTA:
A thousand thanks, Signior Gremio. Welcome, good Cambio. *[to Tranio]* But, gentle
sir, you seem to be a stranger. May I
be so bold as to inquire what you're doing
here?

TRANIO:
Pardon me sir, it is I who am bold. I
am a stranger here and would like to offer
myself as a suitor to your daughter—
to Bianca, fair and virtuous. And, I offer,
for your daughters' educations, this simple
lute and this small packet of Greek and
Latin books—if you accept them, then
they have value.

BAPTISTA:
Lucentio is your name—where from?

TRANIO:
From Pisa sir; son to Vincentio.

BAPTISTA: *[very impressed]*
He is an important man of Pisa; I have
often heard of him. You are very welcome,
sir. *[to Hortensio]* You take the lute,
[to Lucentio] and you take the set of
books—you shall meet your pupils now.
Hello there! *[servant appears]* Boy, take
these gentlemen to my daughters, and tell
them both these are their tutors and to
treat them well. *[exit servant with
Lucentio and Hortensio]*

PETRUCHIO:
Signior Baptista, my business demands
haste. You knew my father well; and through

GREMIO:
Neighbor, to express the like kindness
myself, I freely give unto you this
young scholar, as cunning in Greek,
Latin and other languages as the other
in music. His name is Cambio.

(pushes Luc between himself & Bap)

BAPTISTA:
A thousand thanks, Signior Gremio. Welcome, good Cambio. *[to Tranio]* But, gentle
sir, methinks you walk like a stranger.
May I be so bold to know the cause of your
coming?

*(guides Luc to L of Hor; Luc
& Hor size each other up as
Tra, with Bio following, strides
to R of Bap; others counter R)*

TRANIO:
Pardon me sir, the boldness is mine own,
that being a stranger in this city here,
do make myself a suitor to your daughter—
unto Bianca, fair and virtuous. And,
toward the education of your daughters,
I here bestow a simple instrument and
this small packet of Greek and Latin
books—if you accept them, then their
worth is great.

(bowing to Bap)

*(takes lute & books from Bio,
offers them to Bap)*

(Bap takes the books)

BAPTISTA:
Lucentio is your name—of whence, I pray?

*(opens a book and reads "Luc"
signed on flyleaf)*

TRANIO:
Of Pisa sir; son to Vincentio.

BAPTISTA: *[very impressed]*
A mighty man of Pisa; by report I know
him well. You are very welcome, sir. *[to
Hortensio]* Take you the lute, *[to Lucentio]*
and you the set of books—you shall go
see your pupils presently. Holla, within!
[servant appears] Sirrah, lead these
gentlemen to my daughters, and tell them
both, these are their tutors—bid them
use them well. *[exit servant with Lucentio
and Hortensio]*

(takes lute & hands to Hor)
(hands books to Luc)
*(calls off SL; Servant appears
at SL entrance)*

*(Servant leads them off SL;
they jostle each other to be first)*

PETRUCHIO:
Signior Baptista, my business asketh
haste. You knew my father well; and in

*(Pet shoves Gre; Bio & Tra US
& X to R of Bap; others
counter R)*

him, you know me—sole heir to all his
lands and possessions which I have
increased in value. Then tell me; if I
win your daughter's love, how much is
her dowry?

BAPTISTA:
After I die, half of my land; and when
you marry her, twenty thousand crowns.

PETRUCHIO:
And in exchange, if I die and leave her
widowed, she will get all my land and
the money that it yields. Let's draw up
a special contract.

BAPTISTA:
Yes, when you get that special thing,
that is, her love; for that is everything.

PETRUCHIO:
Why that is nothing; for I tell you,
father, I am as indomitable as she is obstinate;
I am rough and don't woo like a child.

BAPTISTA:
May your wooing go well, and I wish you
good fortune! But be ready for some harsh
words.

[reenter Hortensio]
BAPTISTA:
What's the matter friend, why are you
so pale?

HORTENSIO:
If I look pale, I promise you it is with fear.

BAPTISTA:
What, won't my daughter prove to be a
good musician?

HORTENSIO:
I think she'll sooner prove to be a soldier!

him, me—left solely heir to all his
lands and goods, which I have bettered
rather than decreased. Then tell me; if
I get your daughter's love, what dowry
shall I have with her to wife?

BAPTISTA:
After my death, the one half of my lands;
and, in possession, twenty thousand crowns.

PETRUCHIO:
And for that dowry, I'll assure her of
her widowhood—be it that she survive me—
in all my lands and leases whatsoever. Let
specialties be therefore drawn between us.

BAPTISTA:
Ay, when the special thing is well obtained,
that is, her love; for that is all in all.

PETRUCHIO:
Why that is nothing; for I tell you,
father, I am as peremptory as she proud-
minded; I am rough and woo not like a babe.

BAPTISTA:
Well mayst thou woo, and happy be thy
speed! But be thou armed for some unhappy
words.

[reenter Hortensio]
BAPTISTA:
How now, my friend, why dost thou look
so pale?

*(reenter SL, holding his
hands atop his aching head,
moaning, Xing in a few steps)*

HORTENSIO:
For fear, I promise you, if I look pale.

BAPTISTA:
What, will my daughter prove a good
musician?

HORTENSIO:
I think she'll sooner prove a soldier!

Act Two · Scene 1   vernacular

BAPTISTA:
Why? Can't you instruct her on the lute?

HORTENSIO:
Why no—because she has caused the lute
to destruct on me! I merely told her she
misfingered the frets. "Frets, call you
these?" she said, and struck me on the
head! And through the instrument my noggin
emerged; and there I stood, dazed for
a while, looking through the lute.

PETRUCHIO:
Now by the world, this is a merry gal;
I love her ten times more than I did
before. Oh, how I long to talk with her!

BAPTISTA: *[to Hortensio]*
Well, go with me and begin work with
my younger daughter. Signior Petruchio,
shall I send my daughter Kate to you?

PETRUCHIO:
Please do; I will wait for her here *[exit
Baptista, Gremio, Tranio, Biondello and
Hortensio]* and woo her with spirit when
she comes. Suppose she rants; why then
I'll tell her plainly that she sings as
sweetly as a nightingale. Say that she
sulks; I'll say she looks as cheerful as
morning roses newly washed with dew. If
she tells me to get lost, I'll thank her
as though she'd asked me to stay a week;
and if she denies to wed, I'll ask her
to name the day when we shall be married.
[as Kate enters] But here she comes; and
now Petruchio, speak! Good morning, Kate;
for that's your name I hear.

KATHERINA:
You may have heard, but you're a little
hard of hearing; they call me Katherina;
those who talk of me.

PETRUCHIO:
You lie truly; you are called plain Kate,
and cheerful Kate, and sometimes Kate

BAPTISTA:
Why then thou canst not break her to the lute?

HORTENSIO:
Why no—for she hath broke the lute to
me! I did but tell her she mistook her
frets. "Frets, call you these?" quoth she,
and struck me on the head! And through
the instrument my pate made way; and
there I stood amazed for a while, looking
through the lute.

PETRUCHIO:
Now by the world, it is a lusty wench; I
love her ten times more than e'er I did.
Oh, how I long to have some chat with her!

BAPTISTA: *[to Hortensio]*
Well, go with me, and proceed in practice
with my younger daughter. Signior Petruchio,   *(turning back to Pet)*
shall I send my daughter Kate to you?

PETRUCHIO:
I pray you do; I will attend her here—   *(Bap motions to others; they*
[exit Baptista, Gremio, Tranio, Biondello   *follow Hor off SL, some snigger-*
and Hortensio] and woo her with some   *ing; Bap hands Pet rope & exits*
spirit when she comes. Say that she rail;   *SL; Pet delivers speech DSC*
why then I'll tell her plain, she sings   *while arranging rope & putting*
as sweetly as a nightingale. Say that she   *it in his pocket or belt, takes*
frown; I'll say she looks as clear as   *stools US about five feet, places*
morning roses newly washed with dew. If   *them down about one foot apart)*
she do bid me pack, I'll give her thanks
as though she bid me stay by her a week;
if she deny to wed, I'll crave the day
when I shall be married. *[as Kate enters]*   *(turns, X up to R of C as K*
But here she comes; and now, Petruchio,   *strides on from SL to L of*
speak! Good morrow, Kate; for that's   *C; their eyes meet, they stand*
your name I hear.   *speechless, till Pet finally*
                                                  says "Good morrow...")

KATHERINA:
Well have you heard, but something hard   *(both walk straight DS during*
of hearing; they call me Katherina that do   *their next lines, ending below*
talk of me.   *level of stools)*

PETRUCHIO:
You lie in faith; for you are called plain
Kate, and bonny Kate, and sometimes Kate

the curst; but Kate—the prettiest Kate
in Christendom, my very delicate Kate;
and therefore Kate, listen to this Kate—
having heard your mildness praised in
every town, your virtues spoken of and
much talk of your beauty—yet not as
much as it deserves—I find myself moved
to woo you for my wife.

KATHERINA:
Moved!—very soon—let whoever moved
you here, remove you there! I knew right
off you were a moveable.

PETRUCHIO:
Why, what's a moveable?

KATHERINA:
A piece of furniture.

PETRUCHIO:
You're absolutely right—come, sit on me.

KATHERINA:
Asses are made to bear—and so are you.

PETRUCHIO:
Women are made to bear—and so are you.

KATHERINA:
No such ass as you, if you mean me.

PETRUCHIO:
Come on you wasp, in truth, you are too
angry.

KATHERINA:
If I am waspish, you had best beware my sting.

PETRUCHIO:
My remedy then is to pluck it out.

KATHERINA:
Sure, if the fool could find where it is.

Act Two·Scene 1 **original abridged**	Act Two·Scene 1 **stage directions**

the curst; but Kate—the prettiest Kate
in Christendom, my super-dainty Kate; and
therefore Kate, take this of me Kate—
hearing thy mildness praised in every
town, thy virtues spoke of and thy beauty
sounded—yet not do deeply as to thee
belongs—myself am moved to woo thee for
my wife.

(Pet X to K, kneel on R knee)

KATHERINA:
Moved!—in good time—let him that
moved you hither, remove you hence! I
knew you at the first, you were a moveable.

PETRUCHIO:
Why, what's a moveable?

KATHERINA:
A joint-stool.

PETRUCHIO:
Thou hast hit it—come, sit on me.

*(takes K hand, pulls her down
to sit on his L knee)*

KATHERINA:
Asses are made to bear—and so are you.

(looking him in the eye)

PETRUCHIO:
Women are made to bear—and so are you.

KATHERINA:
No such jade as you if me you mean.

*(stands, pushes Pet; he falls
back; she stands there)*

PETRUCHIO:
Come, come, you wasp, in faith, you are
too angry.

(getting up)

KATHERINA:
If I be waspish, best beware my sting.

PETRUCHIO:
My remedy is then to pluck it out.

KATHERINA:
Ay, if the fool could find it where it lies.

*(folding her arms across her
chest)*

Act Two · Scene 1   vernacular

PETRUCHIO:
Everybody knows where a wasp wears his
sting—in his tail.

KATHERINA:
In his tongue.

PETRUCHIO:
Whose tongue?

KATHERINA:
Yours, if you're just going to talk of tales;
and so farewell.

PETRUCHIO:
What with my tongue in your tail? No,
come back. Good Kate, I am a gentleman.

KATHERINA:
I'll test that. *[she slaps him]*

PETRUCHIO:
I swear I'll slap you if you hit me again.

KATHERINA:
If you hit me, you're no gentleman.

PETRUCHIO:
Oh come on Kate, you musn't look
so sour.

KATHERINA:
I always do when I see a crab.

PETRUCHIO:
There's no crab here, and therefore don't
look sour.

KATHERINA:
There is, there is.

PETRUCHIO:
Then show it to me.

KATHERINA:
If I had a mirror, I would.

Act Two·Scene 1 **original abridged**

PETRUCHIO:
Who knows not where a wasp does wear his sting?—In his tail.

KATHERINA:
In his tongue.

PETRUCHIO:
Whose tongue?

KATHERINA:
Yours, if you talk of tales; and so farewell.

(starts toward SL exit)

PETRUCHIO:
What, with my tongue in your tail? Nay, come again. Good Kate, I am a gentleman.

(she stops abruptly & turns back to him)

KATHERINA:
That I'll try. *[she slaps him]*

(X to him, slaps* him with her left hand; he grabs her left arm with his R hand)

PETRUCHIO:
I swear I'll cuff you, if you strike again.

(after line, K swings at him with R hand; Pet catches it with his left hand)

KATHERINA:
If you strike me you are no gentleman.

PETRUCHIO:
Nay, come Kate, come, you must not look so sour.

(kisses her hands & lets go of them)

KATHERINA:
It is my fashion when I see a crab.

(wiping kisses from her hands)

PETRUCHIO:
Why here's no crab, and therefore look not sour.

KATHERINA:
There is, there is.

PETRUCHIO:
Then show it me.

KATHERINA:
Had I a glass, I would.

(miming a mirror)

PETRUCHIO:
What, do you mean my face?

KATHERINA:
Very good for a such a young 'un.

PETRUCHIO:
Now by Saint George, I am too young for
you.

KATHERINA:
Even so you're withered.

PETRUCHIO:
It's with cares.

KATHERINA:
I couldn't care less.

PETRUCHIO:
Now listen Kate—truly, there's no way out.

KATHERINA:
You'll be sorry if I stay; I'll punch
you out.

PETRUCHIO:
No, not a chance; I think you're very
gentle. I was told you were rough and
coy and sullen, but now I find that's
all a lie; for you are pleasant, playful,
very courteous, gentle, soft and affable.
Why is it said that Kate has a limp? You
are not lame.

KATHERINA:
Where did you learn all this fine speech?

PETRUCHIO:
I made it up—aren't I wise?

KATHERINA:
Barely wise enough to come in out of the
cold.

Act Two·Scene 1 **original abridged**	Act Two·Scene 1 **stage directions**

PETRUCHIO:
What, you mean my face?

KATHERINA:
Well aimed of such a young one.

PETRUCHIO:
Now, by Saint George, I am too young for you.

KATHERINA:
Yet you are withered.

PETRUCHIO:
'Tis with cares..

KATHERINA:
I care not.

(she starts to leave SL)

PETRUCHIO:
Nay, hear you Kate—in sooth, you 'scape not so.

(Pet runs to SL exit to block her way)

KATHERINA:
I chafe you, if I tarry; let me go.

(trying to get past him)

PETRUCHIO:
No, not a whit; I find you passing gentle. 'Twas told me you were rough and coy and sullen, and now I find report a very liar; for thou art pleasant, gamesome, passing courteous, gentle, soft and affable. Why does the world report that Kate doth limp? Thou dost not halt.

(he grabs her by the shoulders, backs her to L stool, seats her by the word "pleasant," stool lazzi)*

KATHERINA:
Where did you study all this goodly speech?

(hopping, holding her R foot)

PETRUCHIO:
It is extempore—am I not wise?

(still seated)

KATHERINA:
Yes; keep you warm.

PETRUCHIO:
Ah sweet Katherine, and when I do, I mean
to warm myself in your bed! Therefore,
leaving aside all this chat, and putting
it plainly: your father has consented
that you shall be my wife; your dowry
is agreed on; and, like it or not, I will
marry you! For by this light, by which
I see your beauty—your beauty that makes
me like you so—you must be married to
no man but me; for I was born to tame
you, Kate. Here comes your father; do
not deny me—for I must and will have
Katherine as my wife.

[reenter Baptista, Gremio and Tranio]
BAPTISTA:
Now, Signior Petruchio, how did it go
with my daughter?

PETRUCHIO:
How could it go but well, sir? It's
impossible for me to fail.

BAPTISTA:
Why how now, daughter Katherine? Are you
upset?

KATHERINA: *[furious]*
You call me daughter? Oh, you have shown
a true fatherly regard, to wish me wed
to a half-lunatic, eccentric wild man
and foul-mouthed jerk!

PETRUCHIO:
Father, this is how it is—you and everyone
else who's talked of her, has misspoken;
if she is curst, it's all for show—
because she's not stubborn, but modest as a
dove; she's not hot-tempered, but temperate
as the morn; and in conclusion, we have
gotten on so well together, that this Sunday
will be our wedding day.

KATHERINA:
I'll see you hanged on Sunday first!

Act Two·Scene 1 **original abridged**	Act Two·Scene 1 **stage directions**
PETRUCHIO: Marry, so I mean sweet Katherine, in thy bed! And therefore, setting all this chat aside, thus in plain terms: your father hath consented that you shall be my wife; your dowry 'greed on; and, will you, nill you, I will marry you! For by this light, whereby I see thy beauty–thy beauty that doth make me like thee well–thou must be married to no man but me; for I am he am born to tame you, Kate. Here comes your father; never make denial–I must and will have Katherine to my wife.	*(rises, takes out rope, rope lazzi*)* *(on "marry you," K opens her mouth to protest; Pet stuffs handkerchief in her mouth*)* *(Pet X DR, holding rope; K hops along behind making muffled protests)*
[reenter Baptista, Gremio and Tranio] BAPTISTA: Now, Signior Petruchio, how speed you with my daughter?	*(they enter from SL, Tra & Gre on either side of Bap; they stop LC)*
PETRUCHIO: How but well sir–how but well? It were impossible that I should speed amiss.	*(Pet X up to R of C with K hopping along behind)*
BAPTISTA: Why how now, daughter Katherine? In your dumps?	*(X to L of C)*
KATHERINA: *[furious]* Call you me daughter? You have showed a tender fatherly regard, to wish me wed to one half lunatic, a mad-cap ruffian and swearing Jack!	*(spits out handkerchief)*
PETRUCHIO: Father, 'tis thus–yourself and all the world that talked of her, have talked amiss; if she be curst, it is for policy– for she's not froward, but modest as the dove; she is not hot, but temperate as the morn; and to conclude, we have 'greed so well together, that upon Sunday is the wedding day.	*(picks up handkerchief, puts it back in her mouth; K makes muffled protests during this speech)*
KATHERINA: I'll see thee hanged on Sunday first!	*(handkerchief still in her mouth)*

Act Two · Scene 1   **vernacular**

GREMIO:
Oh Petruchio! She says she'll see you
hanged first.

PETRUCHIO:
Be patient, gentlemen, we made a bargain
between us when we were alone, that she
will still act curst in the company of
others. I tell you, it's incredible to
believe how much she loves me. Give me
your hand Kate. I will go to Venice, to
buy clothing for the wedding. You prepare
the feast, father, and invite the guests.

BAPTISTA:
I don't know what to say—but give me
your hands. God send you joy, Petruchio,
you're engaged!

GREMIO/TRANIO:
Amen, to that; we are the witnesses.

PETRUCHIO:
Father and wife and gentlemen, adieu;
I will go to Venice; Sunday's almost here
—we will have rings and things and fine
array; and kiss me Kate! *[he kisses her]*
We will be married on Sunday. *[Kate and
Petruchio exit]*

GREMIO:
Was ever an engagement arranged so quickly?
But now Baptista, about your younger daughter;
this is the day we have long awaited. I
am your neighbor and was her suitor first.

TRANIO:
And I am someone that loves Bianca more
than thoughts can even guess.

GREMIO:
Youngster, you can't love so dearly as I!

TRANIO:
Oldster, your love would freeze her!

Act Two · Scene 1 **original abridged**	Act Two · Scene 1 **stage directions**

GREMIO:
Hark Petruchio! She says she'll see thee hanged first.

(stepping in a little, he translates K's muffled speech)

PETRUCHIO:
Be patient, gentlemen, 'tis bargained 'twixt us twain, being alone, that she shall still be curst in company. I tell you, 'tis incredible to believe how much she loves me. Give me thy hand Kate. I will unto Venice, to buy apparel 'gainst the wedding day. Provide the feast, father and bid the guests.

(takes hold of her hand which is still confined by rope)

BAPTISTA:
I know not what to say—but give me your hands. God send you joy, Petruchio, 'tis a match!

(Bap X US between them, takes hold of their hands as Gre & Tra X DR & DL of K & Pet, watching as referees)

GREMIO AND TRANIO:
Amen, say we; we will be witnesses.

PETRUCHIO:
Father and wife and gentlemen, adieu; I will to Venice; Sunday comes apace—we will have rings and things and fine array; and, kiss me Kate! *[he kisses her]* We will be married a' Sunday. *[Kate and Petruchio exit]*

(takes handkerchief out of her mouth, kisses her, exits DR as K stamps on floor, letting out a furious grunt, hopping off to exit SL; others watch, amazed)

GREMIO:
Was ever match clapped up so suddenly? But now Baptista, to your younger daughter; now is the day we long have looked for. I am your neighbor and was suitor first.

TRANIO:
And I am one that love Bianca more than thoughts can guess.

GREMIO:
Youngling, thou canst not love so dear as I!

(Gre takes a step to Tra)

TRANIO:
Greybeard, thy love doth freeze!

(Tra takes a step to Gre)

GREMIO:
But yours would fry! It's age that can
nourish.

TRANIO:
But youth that will flourish.

BAPTISTA:
Easy gentlemen; I will settle this discord:
whoever can assure my daughter of the
greatest dower, shall have Bianca's love.
Tell me Signior Gremio, what would you
give her?

GREMIO:
First, as you know, my house in the city
is richly furnished with silver and gold;
wall hangings of crimson tapestries; ivory
money chests, stuffed with crowns; expen-
sive adornments; fine linens; Venetian
gold; pewter and brass; and everything
that belongs in a house. Then, at my farm,
I have a hundred milking cows, a hundred
and twenty fat oxen and everything that
goes with them. I myself am somewhat aged,
I confess; but, if I die tomorrow, all
this is hers, if while I am alive, she
will be only mine.

TRANIO:
Sir, listen to me—I am my father's heir
and only son; if I may have your daughter
for my wife, I'll leave her three or four
houses, as good as any one that Signior
Gremio has; in addition, land that yields
two thousand ducats a year. *[Gremio makes
a noise]* What, have I pinched you, Signior
Gremio?

GREMIO:
Two thousand ducats a year of land! My
land does not amount to that much in all!
But she shall have it; besides a ship
that is now docked in Marseilles. *[Tranio
makes a noise]* What, have I choked you
with a ship?

Act Two · Scene 1 original abridged

Act Two · Scene 1 stage directions

GREMIO:
But thine doth fry! 'Tis age that
nourisheth.

*(Gre & Tra are nose-to-nose
in front of Bap)*

TRANIO:
But youth that flourisheth.

BAPTISTA:
Content you gentlemen; I will compound
this strife: he that can assure my
daughter the greatest dower, shall have
Bianca's love. Say Signior Gremio, what
can you assure her?

(separating them)

GREMIO:
First, as you know, my house within the
city is richly furnished with plate and
gold; hangings of Tyrian tapestry; ivory
coffers, stuffed with crowns; costly
apparel; fine linen; Venice gold; pewter
and brass; and all things that belong to
house or house-keeping. Then, at my farm,
I have a hundred milch-kine, six score fat
oxen and all things answerable to this
portion. Myself am struck in years, I
must confess; and, if I die tomorrow,
this is hers, if whilst I live, she will
be only mine.

*(taking two steps DS, he delivers
this speech straight out,
getting carried away, illustrat-
ing with gestures as much as
possible)*

TRANIO:
Sir, list to me—I am my father's heir,
and only son; if I may have your daughter
to my wife, I'll leave her houses, three
or four, as good as any one old Signior
Gremio has; besides two thousand ducats
by the year of fruitful land. *[Gremio
makes a noise]* What, have I pinched you,
Signior Gremio?

*(steps down on level with Gre,
delivers his offer calmly &
confidently)*

(Gre makes a high-pitched "oow")

GREMIO:
Two thousand ducats by the year of land!
My land amounts not to so much in all!
That she shall have; besides an argosy
that now is lying in Marseilles. *[Tranio
makes a noise]* What, have I choked you
with an argosy?

(Tra makes a condescending "ooh")

Act Two · Scene 1 vernacular

TRANIO:
Gremio, it is well known that my father
has no less than three great ships. These,
I will give her and twice as much as
whatever you offer next!

GREMIO:
I have offered everything; I have no more;
and she can have no more than all I have.

TRANIO:
Why then the maid is mine. Gremio is
outbid.

BAPTISTA:
I must confess your offer is the best;
and if your father will guarantee it,
she is all yours; else—pardon my saying
so—if you die before him, where's her
dower?

TRANIO:
That's a mere detail; he is old, I am young.

BAPTISTA:
Well gentlemen, I have decided:
next Sunday Katherine is to be married.
Now, on the following Sunday, Bianca will
be bride to you, if you can make this
guarantee; if not, to Signior Gremio.
And now I leave and thank you both.
[he exits]

GREMIO:
Adieu, good neighbor. *[exits]*

TRANIO:
My intention is to do right by my master.
So I see no alternative but that acting
Lucentio must find a father—acting
Vincentio! *[exits]*

Act Two·Scene 1 **original abridged**	Act Two·Scene 1 **stage directions**

TRANIO:
Gremio, 'tis known my father hath no less
than three great argosies. These I will
assure her and twice as much whate'er thou
offer'st next!

GREMIO:
Nay, I have offer'd all; I have no more;
and she can have no more than all I have.

TRANIO:
Why then the maid is mine. Gremio is out-
vied.

BAPTISTA: *(to Tra)*
I must confess your offer is the best; and
let your father make her the assurance,
she is your own; else—you must pardon
me—if you should die before him, where's
her dower?

TRANIO:
That's but a cavil; he is old, I young.

BAPTISTA:
Well gentlemen, I am thus resolved: on
Sunday next, Katherine is to be married.
Now, on the Sunday following, shall Bianca
be bride to you, if you make this
assurance; if not, to Signior Gremio.
And so I take my leave and thank you both.
[he exits]   *(exits SL)*

GREMIO:
Adieu, good neighbor. *[exits]*   *(exits DR)*

TRANIO:
'Tis in my head to do my master good. I   *(X DS to stool, puts foot up*
see no reason, but supposed Lucentio must   *on it, rests arms across knee,*
get a father—supposed Vincentio! *[exits]*   *addresses audience, exits DR)*

Act Three · Scene 1 scene description

This scene shows us the disguised suitors vying for Bianca. They obviously have come to dislike each other's attentions toward Bianca, and things are getting testy.

In this scene, we also see Bianca's true colors beginning to emerge. Bianca flatly states that she will not be told what to do and will learn her lessons as she pleases! She instructs Hortensio/Licio to tune his lute and sits down with Lucentio/Cambio to do her Latin.

Lucentio, while pretending to translate the Latin, is actually revealing his identity to Bianca and telling her of his plan to woo her. Bianca takes over the *translation* and tells Lucentio that she is wary of him, but encourages him by telling him not to despair.

She then turns her attentions to Hortensio. He too has a coded list to *translate* for her and also reveals his identity. Bianca is definitely less encouraging to Hortensio.

When a servant comes to tell Bianca to go help Kate get ready for her wedding, Bianca exits, leaving the suspicious suitors eyeing each other.

Act Three · Scene 1 vernacular

[enter Lucentio, Hortensio and Bianca]

LUCENTIO: *[to Hortensio]*
Strummer, stop—you're too pushy, sir.

HORTENSIO:
Brawling brain-boy, get lost, and after
we've spent an hour on our music, you'll
get equal time for your lecture.

LUCENTIO:
Preposterous ass!

HORTENSIO:
Boy!

BIANCA:
Why gentlemen, I won't be on a schedule,
nor limited in time, but I will learn
my lessons as I please. And to stop this
bickering, *[to Lucentio]* let's sit down.
You, *[to Hortensio]* take your instrument
and play for a while; his lecture will
be done before you have finished tuning.

BIANCA:
Where did we leave off?

LUCENTIO:
Here madam: *[reading]* "Hic ibat Simois;
hic est Sigeia tellus; hic steterat Priami
regia celsa senis."

BIANCA:
Translate.

LUCENTIO:
"Hic ibat,"—as I told you before,
"Simois,"—I am Lucentio,
"hic est,"—son to Vincentio of Pisa,
"Sigeia tellus,"—disguised like this
to court you;
"hic steterat,"—and the "Lucentio"

Act Three · Scene 1 **original abridged**	Act Three · Scene 1 **stage directions**
[enter Lucentio, Hortensio and Bianca]	*(Bi enters SL, X to SR stool, sits, while Hor [with lute] and Luc [with book] jostle for spot near Bi; Hor gets other stool, places it L of Bi, sits)* *(Luc X to between them, shoves Hor off stool; Hor lands on floor L, Luc sits on stool)*
LUCENTIO: *[to Hortensio]* Fiddler, forbear—you grow too forward, sir.	
HORTENSIO: Wrangling pedant, give me leave, and when in music we have spent an hour, your lecture shall have leisure for as much.	*(rising, straightening himself up)*
LUCENTIO: Preposterous ass!	*(rising threateningly)*
HORTENSIO: Sirrah!	
BIANCA: Why gentlemen, I'll not be tied to hours, nor 'pointed times, but learn my lessons as I please. And to cut off all strife, *[to Lucentio]* here sit we down. *[to Hortensio]* Take you your instrument, play you the whiles; his lecture will be done ere you have tuned.	*(rising)* *(Bi & Luc sit)* *(Hor X to ladder, sits on lower rung, mimes tuning lute)*
BIANCA: Where left we last?	
LUCENTIO: Here madam: *[reading]* "Hic ibat Simois; hic est Sigeia tellus; hic steterat Priami regia celsa senis."	*(opening book)*
BIANCA: Construe them.	
LUCENTIO: "Hic ibat,"—as I told you before, "Simois,"—I am Lucentio, "hic est,"—son unto Vincentio of Pisa, "Sigeia tellus,"—disguised thus to get your love; "Hic steterat,"—and that "Lucentio" that	*(reading Latin aloud, whispering* his "translation," pulls disquise off, "reveals" himself, replaces it quickly)*

who pretends to woo,
"Priami,"—is my servant Tranio.

HORTENSIO:
Madam, my instrument's in tune.

BIANCA:
Let's hear. *[he strums the lute]* Oh yuck,
the treble's off.

LUCENTIO:
Spit in the hole and try again.

BIANCA: *[back to Lucentio]*
Now let me see if I can translate it.
"Hic ibat Simois,"—I don't know you;
"hic est Sigeia tellus,"—I don't trust you;
"hic steterat Priami,"—be careful he
doesn't hear us;
"regia,"—don't presume too much;
"celsa senis,"—yet don't despair.

HORTENSIO:
Madam, it's now in tune. *[he strums]*

LUCENTIO:
All but the base.

HORTENSIO:
The base is fine. *[aside]* I swear on my
life, that rascal is courting my love.

BIANCA:
I may come to believe you, but I'm still
doubtful.

LUCENTIO:
Doubt me not.

BIANCA:
But enough. Now Licio, to you.

HORTENSIO: *[to Lucentio]*
Go for a walk and leave us alone.

comes a wooing,
"Priami,"—is my man Tranio.

HORTENSIO:
Madam, my instrument's in tune.

(Xing to SR of Bi)

BIANCA:
Let's hear. *[he strums the lute]* Oh fie,
the treble jars.

LUCENTIO:
Spit in the hole man and tune again.

(Hor stalks back to ladder)

BIANCA: *[back to Lucentio]*
Now let me see if I can construe it.
"Hic ibat Simois,"—I know you not;
"hic est Sigeia tellus,"—I trust you not;
"hic steterat Priami,"—take heed he hear
us not;
"regia,"—presume not;
"celsa senis,"—despair not.

*(taking book, reading Latin
aloud, whispering "translation")*

(Luc touches her arm)
(Luc removes his hand)
(Bi takes his hand in hers)

HORTENSIO:
Madam, 'tis now in tune. *[he strums]*

*(Hor X to R of Bi, she lets
go of Luc hand)*

LUCENTIO:
All but the base.

HORTENSIO:
The base is right. *[aside]* Now for my
life, the knave doth court my love.

(facing out to audience)

BIANCA:
In time I may believe, yet I mistrust.

*(as though they had been
discussing a fine point of Latin)*

LUCENTIO:
Mistrust not.

BIANCA:
But let it rest. Now Licio, to you.

(handing book to Luc)

HORTENSIO: *[to Lucentio]*
You may go walk and give me leave awhile.

(X above Bi to Luc)

LUCENTIO: *[aside]*
Well, I'd better stay and watch because
unless I'm mistaken, our fine musician
is becoming amorous.

HORTENSIO:
Madam, before you touch the instrument,
I must begin with basics; and teach you
scales. There they are in writing.

BIANCA:
Why, I learned my scales ages ago.

HORTENSIO:
But read the scales of Hortensio!

BIANCA: *[reading]*
"Scales,—I am the basis of all harmony,
A re,—to tell you of Hortensio's passion;
B mi,—Bianca, take him for your lord,
C fa,—who loves you so completely."
You call these scales? Pshh, I don't like it.

SERVANT: *[entering]*
Mistress, your father says to leave your
books and help your sister. You know
tomorrow is her wedding day.

BIANCA:
Farewell sweet masters, both of you; I
must go. *[she exits]*

LUCENTIO:
Truly mistress, then I have no reason
to stay. *[he exits]*

HORTENSIO:
But I have a reason to spy on this scholar;
I think he looks lovesick. *[Hortensio
and servant exit]*

Act Three · Scene 1 **original abridged**	Act Three · Scene 1 **stage directions**

LUCENTIO: *[aside]*
Well, I must wait and watch, for but I
be deceived, our fine musician groweth
amorous.

*(rises, X to DLC as Hor is
getting settled on stool; says
line then X to ladder, sits)*

HORTENSIO:
Madam, before you touch the instrument, I
must begin with rudiments of art; to teach
you gamut. And there it is in writing.

(hands her paper)

BIANCA:
Why, I am past my gamut long ago.

HORTENSIO:
Yet read the gamut of Hortensio!

*(pulls off disquise to "reveal"
himself, replaces it quickly)*

BIANCA: *[reading]*
"Gamut,—I am the ground of all accord,
A re,—to plead Hortensio's passion;
B mi,—Bianca, take him for thy lord,
C fa,—that loves with all affection."
Call you this gamut? Tut, I like it not.

(hands paper back to Hor)

SERVANT: *[entering]*
Mistress, your father prays you leave
your books and help your sister. You
know tomorrow is the wedding day.

(runs on from SL to L of Hor)

BIANCA:
Farewell sweet masters, both; I must
be gone. *[she exits]*

*(rises, X below Hor to exit
SL)*

LUCENTIO:
'Faith mistress, then I have no cause to
stay. *[he exits]*

(exits UL)
*(as Hor comes DS to address
audience, Servant X to ladder,
reveals "Town Square"; as Hor
exits UL, servant gets stools,
exits SL)*

HORTENSIO:
But I have cause to pry into this pedant;
methinks he looks as though he were in
love. *[Hortensio and servant exit]*

Act Three · Scene 2 scene description

It is Sunday, the wedding day of Kate and Petruchio, and the groom is overdue. Tranio stands up for Petruchio saying that he has a reputation for honesty and wisdom, but poor Kate is obviously humiliated and distraught, and we now see this curst shrew run off weeping!

Biondello comes running on with news that Petruchio is about to appear and proceeds to describe his outrageous attire.

When Petruchio comes in, Baptista and Tranio try to talk him into changing into something more appropriate for the ceremony, but Petruchio refuses, stating that Kate is marrying him, not his clothing. He then strides off to the church.

Tranio takes this opportunity to fill Lucentio in on his plan to get a man to impersonate Vincentio and give the required guarantees to Baptista so that Lucentio will be able to marry Bianca. Lucentio tells Tranio that he has considered eloping with Bianca but that Hortensio watches her so closely that it would be impossible. Tranio tells him not to worry—all will work out well.

Gremio then comes back from the church and reports what happened during the wedding ceremony. According to him, Petruchio is even more curst than Kate. He says that Petruchio shouted his responses to the priest and acted as though he were carousing with his pals rather than participating in a formal marriage ceremony.

When the rest of the wedding party appears, Petruchio announces that he and Kate must depart immediately. Kate is outraged. A wedding feast has been prepared, and she is not about to miss her party. She and Petruchio have a battle of wills, which Petruchio wins by pretending to fight off the wedding guests to protect Kate. He then literally carries Kate off. Once again, the stunned onlookers stand by as Kate and Petruchio depart.

Act Three · Scene 2   vernacular

[enter Baptista, Tranio, Katherina, Bianca and Lucentio]

BAPTISTA: *[speaking to Tranio]*
Signior Lucentio, this is the day that Katherine and Petruchio should be married, and yet we've heard nothing of our son-in-law. What do you say to our shame.

KATHERINA: *[very upset]*
My shame. I told you he was a madman, who wooed in haste and intends to wed at his leisure.

TRANIO:
Be patient good Katherine, and Baptista too; on my life, Petruchio means well, whatever it is that keeps him away.
Though he may be blunt, he is very wise; though he's a little crazy, yet he's honest.

KATHERINA:
Would that Katherine had never seen him, though! *[exits weeping followed by Bianca]*

BAPTISTA:
Go on girl; I can't blame you for weeping now; such an insult would try a saint's patience, much less a shrew like you.

BIONDELLO: *[entering]*
Masters, news! Petruchio's coming!

BAPTISTA:
When will he be here?

BIONDELLO:
When he stands where I am and sees you there.

TRANIO:
But, what's the news?

BIONDELLO:
Why, Petruchio is coming, in a new hat and an old jacket; a pair of old pants; a pair of boots, one buckled, the other laced; and an old rusty sword with a broken handle.

Act Three · Scene 2 **original abridged**	Act Three · Scene 2 **stage directions**
[enter Baptista, Gremio, Tranio, Katherina, Bianca and Lucentio]	*(Bap enters UC, Tra on his R; they X RC, looking off DR; Gre & Luc follow Xing LC to look off DL; K & Bi enter last, Xing slowly D so that all end up in a sort of semicircle)*
BAPTISTA: *[speaking to Tranio]* Signior Lucentio, this is the day that Katherine and Petruchio should be married, and yet we hear not of our son-in-law. What says Lucentio to this shame of ours?	
KATHERINA: *[very upset]* No shame but mine. I told you he was a frantic fool, who wooed in haste and means to wed at leisure.	*(steps DC on level with Bap)*
TRANIO: Patience good Katherine, and Baptista too; upon my life, Petruchio means well, whatever fortune stays him from his word. Though he be blunt, I know him passing wise; though he be merry, yet he's honest.	
KATHERINA: Would Katherine had never seen him, though! *[exits weeping followed by Bianca]*	*(exit DL)*
BAPTISTA: Go girl; I cannot blame thee now to weep; for such an injury would vex a saint, much less a shrew of thy impatient humour.	*(Xing C, looking DL after his daughters)*
BIONDELLO: *[entering]* Masters, news! Petruchio's coming!	*(enters DR Xing in a little)*
BAPTISTA: When will he be here?	*(Xing DS a few steps)*
BIONDELLO: When he stands where I am and sees you there.	
TRANIO: But, to thy news.	*(Xing DS on level with Bap)*
BIONDELLO: Why, Petruchio is coming, in a new hat and an old jerkin; a pair of old breeches; a pair of boots, one buckled, another laced; and an old rusty sword with a broken hilt.	*(turning out a little toward audience)*

Act Three · Scene 2   vernacular

BAPTISTA:
Who comes with him?

BIONDELLO:
Oh sir, his servant; looking like some monster; and not at all like a gentleman's servant.

TRANIO: *[to Baptista]*
It's some strange whim that makes him do this.

BAPTISTA:
I am glad he comes, however he comes.

[enter Petruchio and Grumio]
PETRUCHIO:
Come on, where are these brave hearts? Who's here?

BAPTISTA:
You are welcome sir.

PETRUCHIO:
And yet I come not well.

TRANIO:
Not as well dressed as I wish you were.

PETRUCHIO:
But where is Kate? Where is my lovely bride? Gentlemen, you're frowning. Why do you look as if you saw a comet or some strange vision?

BAPTISTA:
Why sir, you know that this is your wedding day. First we were sad, because we were afraid you weren't coming and now we're even sadder because you show up so inappropriately. Pshh, get rid of these clothes!

TRANIO:
And tell us what kept you so long and sent you here so unlike yourself?

BAPTISTA:
Who comes with him?

BIONDELLO:
Oh sir, his lackey; a monster, a very monster in apparel; and not like a gentleman's lackey.

TRANIO: *[to Baptista]*
'Tis some odd humor pricks him to this fashion.

BAPTISTA:
I am glad he is come, howsoe'er he comes.

[enter Petruchio and Grumio]
PETRUCHIO:
Come, where be these gallants? Who's at home?

BAPTISTA:
You are welcome sir.

PETRUCHIO:
And yet I come not well.

TRANIO:
Not so well apparelled as I wish you were.

PETRUCHIO:
But where is Kate? Where is my lovely bride? Gentles, methinks you frown. Wherefore gaze this goodly company, as if they saw some comet or unusual prodigy?

BAPTISTA:
Why sir, you know this is your wedding day. First were we sad, fearing you would not come; now sadder, that you come so unprovided. Fie, doff this habit!

TRANIO:
And tell us what hath so long detained you and sent you hither so unlike yourself?

(enter from DR with great bravado, X to ladder, Pet climbs to top & sits as Gru stands at foot of it; Bio & Tra counter left; all watch amazed)

(Bap X US on level with Pet)

PETRUCHIO:
It's too boring to talk about. Just be
glad I'm here. But, where is Kate? It's
time we were at church.

TRANIO:
Don't see your bride looking like this,
go to my room, put on some of my clothes.

PETRUCHIO:
I don't think so; I'll see her like this.

BAPTISTA:
But I trust, this isn't how you'll marry her.

PETRUCHIO:
Yes truly, just like this; therefore enough
talk; she's marrying me, not my clothes.
But what kind of fool am I, to be chatting
with you, when I should greet my bride,
and seal the bargain with a loving kiss!
[Petruchio and Grumio exit]

BAPTISTA:
I'll go after him and see what happens.
[exit Baptista and Gremio]

TRANIO: *[to Lucentio]*
Sir, as I told you before, I'm looking
for a man—whatever he is, it doesn't
really matter—to be Vincentio of Pisa;
and to make a guarantee of even more than
I have already promised. This way, you
can get your wish and marry sweet Bianca
with consent.

LUCENTIO:
If it weren't for my fellow schoolmaster
watching every step Bianca takes, I think
it would be a good idea to elope.

TRANIO:
That's worth looking into—we'll watch
for an opportunity. We'll outwit old man
Gremio, that nosey father Minola, the
silly musician, lovesick Licio; all for

PETRUCHIO:
Tedious it were to tell. Sufficeth, I am
come. But, where is Kate? 'Tis time we
were at church.

(descending ladder)

TRANIO:
See not your bride in these robes, go
to my chamber, put on clothes of mine.

(Xing to Pet a step)

PETRUCHIO:
Not I, believe me; thus I'll visit her.

BAPTISTA:
But thus, I trust, you will not marry her.

PETRUCHIO:
Good sooth, even thus; therefore have done
with words; to me she's married, not unto
my clothes. But what a fool am I to chat
with you, when I should bid good morrow to
my bride, and seal the title with a lovely
kiss! *[Petruchio and Grumio exit]*

(strides off DL)

BAPTISTA:
I'll after him and see the event of this.
[exit Baptista and Gremio]

(Bap exits DL, Gre following)

TRANIO: *[to Lucentio]*
Sir, as I before imparted, I am to get
a man—whate'er he be, it skills not
much—and he shall be Vincentio of Pisa;
and make assurance, here in Padua, of
greater sums than I have promised. So
shall you enjoy your hope and marry
sweet Bianca with consent.

*(Tra, Luc, & Bio meet C—Tra
C, Luc SL of him, Bio SR)*

LUCENTIO:
Were it not that my fellow schoolmaster
doth watch Bianca's steps so narrowly,
'twere good methinks, to steal our marriage.

TRANIO:
That we mean to look into and watch our
vantage in this business. We'll over-reach
the greybeard, Gremio, the narrow-prying
father, Minola, the quaint musician,

Act Three · Scene 2 — vernacular

the sake of my master, Lucentio! *[Gremio enters]* Signior Gremio, are you coming from church?

GREMIO:
As willingly as I ever came from school.

TRANIO:
Are the bride and groom coming?

GREMIO:
I'll say! He's a grumbling groom.

TRANIO:
Worse than she? That's not possible.

GREMIO:
Why he's a devil, a devil, a very fiend.

TRANIO:
Why she's a devil, a devil, the devil's mother.

GREMIO:
Oh pooh! She's a lamb, a dove, a little dear compared to him. I tell you sir Lucentio; when the priest asked if he would take Katherine for his wife, "You're god-damned right," he said; so loud, that the stunned priest dropped the bible!

TRANIO:
What did the girl say?

GREMIO:
She trembled and shook; he stamped and swore. Then after the ceremony was done, he calls for wine: "To your health," he says, as if he were carousing with a bunch of sailors after a storm. Then, he grabbed the bride around the neck, and kissed her lips with such a noisy *smmmack,* that when they parted, the whole church echoed. There's never been such a mad marriage.

[enter Petruchio, Katherina, Bianca, Baptista and Grumio]

amorous Licio; all for my master's sake,
Lucentio! *[Gremio enters]* Signior Gremio,
came you from the church?

GREMIO:
As willingly as e'er I came from school.

TRANIO:
And is the bride and groom coming?

GREMIO:
Indeed! 'Tis a grumbling groom.

TRANIO:
Curster than she? Why 'tis impossible.

GREMIO:
Why he's a devil, a devil, a very fiend.

TRANIO:
Why, she's a devil, a devil, the devil's dam.

GREMIO:
Tut! She's a lamb, a dove, a fool to him.
I'll tell you sir Lucentio; when the
priest should ask if Katherine should
be his wife, "Ay, by gogs-wouns," quoth
he; so loud, that all amazed, the priest
let fall the book!

TRANIO:
What said the wench?

GREMIO:
Trembled and shook; he stamped and swore.
But after many ceremonies done, he calls
for wine: "A health," quoth he, as if he
had been aboard, carousing to his mates
after a storm. Then, he took the bride
about the neck, and kissed her lips with
such a clamorous smack, that at the
parting, all the church did echo. Such
a mad marriage never was before.

*[enter Petruchio, Katherina, Bianca,
Baptista and Grumio]*

*(enters DL, X to Tra; Luc counter
L)*

*(mimicking what he has seen
& heard)*

*(Pet leads K on DL; Bap, Bi,
& Gru follow; Luc, Gre, Tra*

Act Three · Scene 2   **vernacular**

PETRUCHIO:
Gentlemen and friends, I thank you for
your trouble. I know you're expecting
to dine with me now, and have prepared
a great wedding banquet; but, I'm in a
hurry to get going, and therefore now
I mean to leave.

BAPTISTA:
Is it possible you will leave tonight?

PETRUCHIO:
I must leave today, before night comes.
Good people, I thank you all who have
watched me give myself away to this
patient, sweet and virtuous wife. Dine
with my father, drink a toast to me;
for now I must leave. Good-by to you all.

TRANIO:
Let us entreat you to stay till after dinner.

PETRUCHIO:
It may not be.

GREMIO:
Let me entreat you.

PETRUCHIO:
It cannot be.

KATHERINA:
Let me entreat you.

PETRUCHIO:
I am content.

KATHERINA:
Are you content to stay?

PETRUCHIO:
I am content that you should entreat me to
stay; but I won't stay, entreat me how you may.

KATHERINA:
No, then do what you may, I won't go today;
no, nor tomorrow. The door is open sir,

Act Three·Scene 2 original abridged

Act Three·Scene 2 stage directions

PETRUCHIO:
Gentlemen and friends, I thank you for your pains. I know you think to dine with me today, and have prepared great store of wedding cheer; but, my haste doth call me hence, and therefore here I mean to take my leave.

& Bio clear to RC; Pet X to C with K; Bap, Bi, & Gru stay LC)

BAPTISTA:
Is't possible you will away tonight?

(stepping in to L of K)

PETRUCHIO:
I must away today, before night come. Honest company, I thank you all that have beheld me give away myself to this most patient, sweet and virtuous wife. Dine with my father, drink a health to me; for I must hence. Farewell to you all.

(holding K's hand, Pet takes a step toward DR as Tra steps forward into his path)

TRANIO:
Let us entreat you stay till after dinner.

PETRUCHIO:
It may not be.

GREMIO:
Let me entreat you.

(Gre X to between Pet & Tra)

PETRUCHIO:
It cannot be.

KATHERINA:
Let me entreat you.

PETRUCHIO:
I am content.

KATHERINA:
Are you content to stay?

PETRUCHIO:
I am content you shall entreat me stay; but yet not stay, entreat me how you can.

KATHERINA:
Nay then, do what thou canst, I will not go today; no, nor tomorrow. The door is

(breaks away, X DLC)

there lies your way; as for me, I won't
go till I'm ready.

PETRUCHIO:
Oh Kate, please don't be angry.

KATHERINA:
I will be angry! What are you going to
do about it? Father, not a word. Gentlemen,
forward to the bridal dinner. I see a
woman may be made a fool of, if she hasn't
the spirit to resist.

PETRUCHIO:
They shall go Kate, as you command. Obey
the bride; go to the feast, revel, be
madcap and merry. But as for my lovely
Kate, she must go with me. *[to Kate who
is furious]* Don't you dare look angry,
nor stamp, nor fret; I will command that
which is mine. Here she is, touch her
if you dare. Grumio, draw your weapon,
we are surrounded with thieves; rescue
your mistress, if you're a man. Don't
be afraid, sweet girl, they shall not
lay a finger on you; I'd protect you even
if there were a million. *[exit Petruchio,
Kate and Grumio]*

BAPTISTA:
Let them go!

TRANIO:
Of all the wild weddings, there never
was one like this!

LUCENTIO:
Mistress, what's your opinion of your sister?

BIANCA:
That being mad herself, she's madly mated.

GREMIO:
I promise, Petruchio has been Kated!

BAPTISTA:
Neighbors and friends, come, let's go.
[all exit]

Act Three · Scene 2 original abridged

open sir, there lies your way; for me,
I'll not be gone till I please myself.

PETRUCHIO:
Oh Kate, prithee be not angry.

KATHERINA:
I will be angry! What hast thou to do?
Father, be quiet. Gentlemen, forward to
the bridal dinner. I see, a woman may be
made a fool, if she had not a spirit to
resist.

PETRUCHIO:
They shall go forward Kate, at thy
command. Obey the bride; go to the feast,
revel, be mad and merry. But for my bonny
Kate, she must with me. *[to Kate who is
furious]* Nay, look not big, nor stamp, nor
fret; I will be master of what is mine own
Here she stands, touch her whoever dare.
Grumio, draw thy weapon, we are beset with
thieves; rescue thy mistress, if thou be
a man. Fear not, sweet wench, they shall
not touch thee, Kate; I'll buckler thee
against a million. *[exit Petruchio, Kate
and Grumio]*

BAPTISTA:
Let them go!

TRANIO:
Of all mad matches, never was the like!

LUCENTIO:
Mistress, what's your opinion of your sister?

BIANCA:
That being mad herself, she's madly mated.

GREMIO:
I warrant him, Petruchio is Kated!

BAPTISTA:
Neighbors and friends, come, let's go.
[all exit]

Act Three · Scene 2   stage directions

(indicating DR exit)

(Xing DS on level with K)

*(Bap takes a step DS, opens
his mouth; K shuts him up with
her line before he can speak)*

(with arms wide open)

*(all except K, Pet, & Gru start
to X UC; K X threateningly
to Pet; all stop & watch as
Pet draws sword, circles US,
& around threatening all; they
scatter; Pet ends L of K; Gru
draws sword & chases all UC
as Pet lifts K over his shoulder
& carries her off DR; Gru
follows, backing out)*

(Xing DC)

(Xing D to R of Bap)

(Xing D with Bi to L of Bap)

(Xing D to R of Tra)

(all exit UC, following Bap)

Act Four • Scene 1   scene description

We now find ourselves in Petruchio's home. Grumio has just come in out of the cold and is trying to prepare things for the arrival of Petruchio and Kate.

Curtis, one of the other servants in the household, is anxious for information about Petruchio's new wife, and once Grumio assures himself that the household is ready, he proceeds to tell the tale of the journey.

He tells of Kate's horse stumbling and falling, dumping Kate in a mucky spot; of Petruchio blaming Grumio for the mishap and beating him; of Kate's attempt to rescue him from Petruchio; and of the horses running away. The two servants conclude that Petruchio is a worse shrew than Kate.

In comes Kate and Petruchio and we immediately see more examples of the outrageous behavior that Grumio has just described. We also see Kate trying to smooth things over and make peace.

After throwing the tray of food that has been brought in, Petruchio takes Kate off to her bridal chamber where, it is reported, he delivers a speech to her about abstinency.

Petruchio then returns and fills the audience in on his plan. He tells us that he intends to continue in this mode, keeping Kate from eating or sleeping, while telling her that he is doing all this in order to take care of her.

Act Four • Scene 1   vernacular

[enter Grumio]

GRUMIO:
Fie on all mad masters! I've been sent ahead to make a fire, and they are then coming to warm themselves. Hello, hey! Curtis!

CURTIS: *[entering]*
Who's calling so coldly?

GRUMIO:
A piece of ice! A fire good Curtis.

CURTIS:
Is my master and his wife coming, Grumio?

GRUMIO:
Oh yes Curtis, yes. And therefore a fire.

CURTIS:
Is she so hot-tempered a shrew as is reported?

GRUMIO:
She was, good Curtis, before this frost. But you know, winter tames man, woman and beast. Therefore fire—my master and my mistress are almost frozen to death.

CURTIS:
The fire's ready and therefore, good Grumio, what's the news?

GRUMIO:
Where's the cook? Is supper ready, the house neat, cobwebs swept, and everything in order?

CURTIS:
All's ready! and therefore, please, the news!

GRUMIO:
First know that my horse is tired; my master and my mistress have fallen out.

CURTIS:
How?

Act Four · Scene 1 **original abridged**	Act Four · Scene 1 **stage directions**
[enter Grumio] Grumio: Fie on all mad masters! I am sent before to make a fire, and they are coming after to warm them. Holla, hoa! Curtis!	*(Gru enters SL, cold, tired, hungry, trying to warm his hands, X to ladder, sits, shivering on bottom rung, calling loudly)*
CURTIS: *[entering]* Who is that calls so coldly?	*(enters SR with three stools which he sets up in a line just below C)*
GRUMIO: A piece of ice! A fire good Curtis.	*(as soon as Cur realizes it's Gru, he X up to him)*
CURTIS: Is my master and his wife coming, Grumio?	
GRUMIO: Oh, ay Curtis, ay. And therefore fire.	
CURTIS: Is she so hot a shrew as she's reported?	
GRUMIO: She was, good Curtis, before this frost. But thou know'st, winter tames man, woman and beast. Therefore fire—my master and mistress are almost frozen to death.	
CURTIS: There's fire ready and therefore, good Grumio, the news.	*(becoming slightly exasperated)*
GRUMIO: Where's the cook? Is supper ready, the house trimmed, cobwebs swept, and every- thing in order?	*(jumps up, X to LC circling around to check things out, winding up DR of ladder)*
CURTIS: All ready!—and therefore, I pray thee, news!	*(on "All ready," Gru looks down at sign; Cur, chagrined, tears off to reveal "Pet House," stuffs other in pocket, then finishes his line)*
GRUMIO: First know, my horse is tired; my master and my mistress fallen out.	*(Gru, finally satisfied, X to SR stool, sits, followed by Cur who sits on SL stool)*
CURTIS: How?	

Act Four · Scene 1   **vernacular**

GRUMIO:
Out of their saddles and into the dirt—
and thereby hangs a tale.

CURTIS:
Let's hear it, good Grumio.

GRUMIO:
We came down a muddy hill, my master was
riding behind my mistress—

CURTIS: *[interrupting]*
Both on one horse?

GRUMIO:
What's it to you?

CURTIS:
Why, a horse.

GRUMIO:
All right, you tell the tale! But, if
you hadn't interrupted, you might have
heard how her horse fell, with her under
it; you might have heard in how yucky
a place: how she was covered with slime;
how he left her with the horse on her;
how he beat me because her horse had
stumbled; how she waded through the dirt
to pull him off me; how he swore; how
she prayed; how I cried; how the horses
ran away; how I lost my purse, with many
things of value, which shall now be lost
forever.

CURTIS:
By this account, he's a worse shrew than she.

GRUMIO:
Yup; and you'll see for yourself when
he gets here. Is everything ready?

CURTIS:
It's all ready. How near is our master?

GRUMIO:
Almost here.

Act Four·Scene 1   original abridged

Act Four·Scene 1   stage directions

GRUMIO:
Out of their saddles into the dirt—and thereby hangs a tale.

CURTIS:
Let's have it, good Grumio.

(Gru delivers this tale using as many illustrative gestures & sounds as the actor can devise, moving wherever he chooses; Cur listens in rapt attention from stool)

GRUMIO:
We came down a foul hill, my master riding behind my mistress—

CURTIS: *[interrupting]*
Both of one horse?

GRUMIO:
What's that to thee?

CURTIS:
Why, a horse.

GRUMIO:
Tell thou the tale! But, hadst thou not crossed me, thou shouldst have heard how her horse fell, and she under her horse; thou shouldst have heard, in how miry a place: how she was bemoiled; how he left her with the horse upon her; how he beat me because her horse stumbled; how she waded through the dirt to pluck him off me; how he swore; how she prayed; how I cried; how the horses ran away; how I lost my crupper, with many things of worthy memory, which now shall die in oblivion.

CURTIS:
By this reckoning, he is more shrew than she.

(seeing the whole picture Gru has painted)

GRUMIO:
Ay; and that thou shall find when he comes home. Is all ready?

(returning to Cur from wherever he ended up)

CURTIS:
All things is ready. How near is our master?

GRUMIO:
E'en at hand.

Act Four · Scene 1   **vernacular**

PETRUCHIO: *[from offstage]*
Where are these no-counts?

GRUMIO:
I hear my master.

[enter Petruchio and Kate]

PETRUCHIO:
What, no one at the door? No attendance?
No regard? No duty? Where is the foolish
no-count I sent before?

GRUMIO:
Here sir; as foolish as I was before.

PETRUCHIO:
Go on you rascal, go and bring my supper
in. *[Grumio exits]* Sit down, Kate. *[yelling
after Grumio]* Come on, when? Good sweet
Kate, cheer up. *[to Curtis]* Take off my
boots, you rogue, you villain. Get out,
you rogue! You hurt my foot. Take that
and do the other one right. Be happy,
Kate. *[to Curtis]* Bring us some water
here! *[Curtis exits]* Where are my slippers?
Where's the water? *[Curtis reappears]*
Come on Kate, and wash. *[to Curtis]* You
moron! Will you let it spill?

KATHERINA:
Please, be patient; it was an accident.

PETRUCHIO:
A beetle-headed, flap-eared no-count!
Come on Kate, sit down; I know you must
be hungry. Will you give thanks, sweet
Kate, or shall I? What's this? Mutton!

GRUMIO:
Ay.

PETRUCHIO:
Who brought it?

GRUMIO:
I.

Act Four • Scene 1 **original abridged**	Act Four • Scene 1 **stage directions**
PETRUCHIO: *[from offstage]* Where be these knaves?	
GRUMIO: I hear my master.	*(Cur runs off SR; Gru runs up to hide behind ladder)*
[enter Petruchio and Katherina] PETRUCHIO: What, no man at door? No attendance? No regard? No duty? Where is the foolish knave I sent before?	*(Pet enters SL, pulling K by the arm, Xing in a few steps)*
GRUMIO: Here sir; as foolish as I was before.	*(popping out from behind ladder)*
PETRUCHIO: Go rascal, go and fetch my supper in. *[Grumio exits]* Sit down, Kate. *[yelling after Grumio]* Why, when I say? Good sweet Kate, be merry. *[to Curtis]* Off with my boots, you rogue, you villain. Out, you rogue! You pluck my foot awry. Take that and mend the plucking of the other. Be merry, Kate. *[to Curtis]* Some water here! *[Curtis exits]* Where are my slippers? Shall I have some water? *[Curtis reappears]* Come Kate, and wash. *[to Curtis]* You villain! Will you let it fall?	*(Gru exit SR; Pet drags K to L stool, seats her, as Cur enters SR warily; Pet sits on SR stool, Cur straddles Pet's outstretched leg facing out; Pet shoves him with his other foot; Cur falls forward, hastily removes other boot, exits with boots SR; Pet shouting after Cur; Cur reenters SR with water X US of C stool; Pet causes water to tip out on K; Pet jumps up, chases Cur DS around stools & off SR)*
KATHERINA: Patience, I pray you; 'twas a fault unwilling.	*(rising)*
PETRUCHIO: A beetle-headed, flap-eared knave! Come Kate, sit down; I know you have a stomach. Will you give thanks, sweet Kate, or else shall I? What's this? Mutton!	*(Pet sits SR stool; K sits SL; Gru enters SR with tray, sets it on C stool; not waiting for answer, Pet bows his head, offers prayer*, looks up, sees meat, goes on)*
GRUMIO: Ay.	*(still above C stool)*
PETRUCHIO: Who brought it?	
GRUMIO: I.	*(his voice quavering)*

PETRUCHIO:
It's burnt! How dare you, numb-skull,
serve it to me like this. There, take
it back, dishes, cups and all.

KATHERINA:
Please, husband, calm down; the meat was
fine, if you could just be satisfied.

PETRUCHIO:
I tell you Kate, it was burnt and dried
up and I'm specifically warned not to
touch it, because it inflames my temper,
it makes me angry; and it's better for
both of us to fast than to eat such over-
roasted flesh. Be patient; tomorrow it
will be corrected, and for tonight, we'll
fast. Come, I will bring you to your bridal
suite. *[exit Petruchio and Kate]*

GRUMIO: *[to the audience]*
Did you ever see anything like this? He's
giving her a taste of her own medicine.
[Curtis reenters] Where is he?

CURTIS:
In her chamber, making a speech about
sexual abstinence to her—and rails and
swears and rates; that she, poor soul,
doesn't know which way to stand, to look,
to speak. Away, away, he's coming!

PETRUCHIO: *[reentering]*
Thus have I shrewdly begun to exercise
my rule, and I hope all will turn out
well. She ate nothing today, nor will
she eat; last night she did not sleep,
and tonight she shall not; as I did with
the meat, I'll find some made-up flaw
about how the bed was made; and I'll fling
the pillow over here, the bolster, there,
the coverlet this way, another way the
sheets—yes, and tell her, amid this
frenzy, that everything I do is humbly
offered in loving care of her. And, to
conclude, she shall stay awake all night.

PETRUCHIO:
'Tis burnt! How durst you villain, serve
it thus to me. There, take it to you,
trenchers, cups and all.

*(Picks up tray, tosses so all
lands US; Gru starts to gather
it all up)*

KATHERINA:
I pray you, husband, be not so disquiet;
the meat was well if you were so contented.

*(reaching across to mollify
Pet)*

PETRUCHIO:
I tell thee Kate, 'twas burnt and dried
away and I expressly am forbid to touch
it, for it engenders choler, planteth
anger; and better it were that both of
us did fast than feed with such over-
roasted flesh. Be patient; tomorrow it
shall be mended, and for this night, we'll
fast. Come, I will bring thee to thy
bridal chamber. *[exit Petruchio and Kate]*

(Pet takes K off SR)

GRUMIO: *[aside]*
Didst ever see the like? He kills her in
her own humour. *[Curtis reenters]*
Where is he?

*(X C with tray & stuff, delivers
aside; Cur enter SR, X to Gru)*

CURTIS:
In her chamber, making a sermon of
continency to her–and rails and swears
and rates; that she, poor soul, knows
not which way to stand, to look, to speak.
Away, away, for he is coming!

*(Gru repeats "continency?"; Cur
nods, repeats "continency," goes
on; hearing Pet coming, Cur
grabs SR stool; Gru with his
tray & stuff, & Cur exit UR
as Pet enters SR; Pet X to DC,
delivers monologue*, standing
or using stools, however actor
prefers)*

PETRUCHIO: *[reentering]*
Thus have I politicly begun my reign, and
'tis my hope to end successfully. She eat
no meat today, nor none shall eat; last
night she slept not, nor tonight she shall
not; as with the meat, some undeserved
fault I'll find about the making of the
bed; and here I'll fling the pillow, there
the bolster, this way the coverlet, another
way the sheets–ay, and amid this hurly, I
intend that all is done in reverend care of her.
And in conclusion, she shall watch all night.

And if she happens to drop off, I'll rail
and brawl, and make such a racket that
I will keep her awake. This is how to
kill a wife with kindness; and this is
how I'll temper her angry, headstrong
nature. If anyone knows a better way to
tame a shrew, tell me now; it would be
a blessing to know. *[exit]*

Act Four · Scene 2 scene description

This scene switches back to the Minola house
in Padua. Tranio is in the process of getting
Hortensio out of the picture. Tranio has obviously
gotten Hortensio to reveal his suspicions about
Bianca and the Latin teacher to him. They hide
themselves and watch as Lucentio and Bianca flirt.

Tranio pretends to be outraged. He and
Hortensio (who has by now revealed his true identity to Tranio) renounce their love for the fickle
Bianca and vow to have nothing further to do with
her. Hortensio announces that he will marry a
wealthy widow, and he leaves.

Tranio fills Lucentio and Bianca in on the good
news. Biondello then arrives saying that he has finally located someone to act the part of the false
Vincentio.

On comes the Pedant. We discover that he is
from Mantua and that he intends to remain in
Padua for a week or two. Tranio quickly makes up a
story saying that the duke has proclaimed a death
sentence on any Mantuans who are found in
Padua. He then says that since the Pedant reminds
him of his father Vincentio, he will save his life by
allowing him to stay at his house and impersonate
Vincentio.

The Pedant gratefully takes him up on his offer,
and they exit with Tranio telling the Pedant about
the marriage assurance that Vincentio must give.

Act Four · Scene 2   vernacular

[enter Bianca, Lucentio, Tranio and Hortensio]
TRANIO: *[pretending to be amazed]*
Is it possible, my friend Licio, that
mistress Bianca loves someone else?

HORTENSIO:
Sir, to prove what I have told you, stand
aside and note how he teaches her. *[they
hide]*

LUCENTIO:
So mistress, are you enjoying that book?

BIANCA:
Master, what are you reading? First tell
me that.

LUCENTIO:
I'm reading that which I practice, "The
Art To Love."

BIANCA:
And sir, let's hope you prove a master
of your art!

LUCENTIO:
While you, my sweet dear, are proving
the mistress of my heart.

TRANIO:
Oh hateful love! Fickle womankind! I tell
you Licio, this is amazing!

And if she chance to nod, I'll
rail and brawl, and with the clamour keep
her still awake. This is a way to kill a
wife with kindness; and thus I'll curb her
mad and headstrong humour. He that knows
better how to tame a shrew, now let him
speak; 'tis charity to show. *[exit]*

(regroups his energy, exits SR)

[enter Bianca, Lucentio, Tranio and Hortensio]
TRANIO: *[pretending to be amazed]*
Is't possible, friend Licio, that mistress
Bianca doth fancy any other?

HORTENSIO:
Sir, to satisfy you in what I have said,
stand by and mark the manner of his teaching. *[they hide]*

LUCENTIO:
Now mistress, profit you in what you read?

BIANCA:
What master, read you? First resolve me
that.

LUCENTIO:
I read that I profess, "The Art To Love."

BIANCA:
And may you prove sir, master of your art!

LUCENTIO:
While you, sweet dear, prove mistress of
my heart.

TRANIO:
Oh despiteful love! Unconstant womankind!
I tell thee Licio, this is wonderful.

*(Bi & Luc enter UC with books,
X to stools, sit—Bi on R—open books,
read, holding books in their outside hands,
holding each other's inside hand;
Tra & Hor enter UC, X to ladder,
whispering; Hor reveals "Town Square"
sign, puts other in pocket, they bring
ladder to above C, "hiding behind"
ladder to "spy")*

(turning to Bi)

(turning to Luc)

*(they let their books drop &
they kiss)*

*(aside to Hor from side of
ladder)*

Act Four · Scene 2   **vernacular**

HORTENSIO:
Let me deceive you no more. I am not Licio,
nor a musician, as I seem to be; but know
sir, that my name is Hortensio.

TRANIO:
Signior Hortensio, I have heard of your
affection for Bianca; and since I have seen
with my own eyes her lewdness, I will, if you
will, renounce Bianca and her love forever.

HORTENSIO:
See how they kiss and court! Signior
Lucentio, shake on it, I vow never to
woo her again.

TRANIO:
And I take an equal oath, never to marry
her. Darn her!

HORTENSIO:
I will marry a wealthy widow, within the next
three days, who has long been in love with me.
And so farewell, Signior Lucentio. *[exits]*

TRANIO:
Mistress Bianca, Hortensio and I have
renounced your love.

LUCENTIO:
Then we are rid of Licio.

TRANIO:
Truly, he'll have a lively widow now.

BIANCA:
God bless him!

BIONDELLO: *[entering]*
Oh master, master, I've been watching
for so long that I'm dog-tired; but I
finally spied an old man coming down the
hill who will serve our purpose.

TRANIO:
What's he like Biondello?

Act Four • Scene 2 **original abridged**	Act Four • Scene 2 **stage directions**

HORTENSIO:
Mistake no more. I am not Licio, nor a
musician, as I seem to be; know sir,
that I am called Hortensio.

*(aside to Tra from side of ladder,
whips off disguise, and puts
it in his pocket)*

TRANIO:
Signior Hortensio, I have heard of your
affection for Bianca; and since mine eyes
are witness of her lightness, I will with
you, forswear Bianca and her love forever.

*(Hor wads up "Pet House" sign
into ball, throws it at Luc
who picks it up, impales it
on his pencil point, hands
this "flower" to Bi; she takes
it, sniffs it, leans over to
kiss Luc again)*

HORTENSIO:
See how they kiss and court! Signior
Lucentio, here is my hand, and here I
vow never to woo her more.

(Hor offers his hand to Tra)

TRANIO:
And here I take the like oath, never to
marry her. Fie on her!

(Tra shakes Hor hand)

HORTENSIO:
I will be married to a wealthy widow, ere
three days pass, which hath long loved me.
And so farewell, Signior Lucentio. *[exits]*

(exits UR)

TRANIO:
Mistress Bianca. I have forsworn you with
Hortensio.

(Xing to Bi & kneeling)

LUCENTIO:
Then we are rid of Licio.

TRANIO:
In faith, he'll have a lusty widow now.

BIANCA:
God give him joy!

BIONDELLO: *[entering]*
Oh master, master, I have watched so long
that I'm dog-weary; but at last I spied
an ancient coming down the hill, will
serve the turn.

*(enters DR, X to R of Tra who
rises)*

TRANIO:
What is he Biondello?

BIONDELLO:
Master, a businessman or a scholar, I'm
not sure; but well-dressed, he walks and looks
like a father.

LUCENTIO:
And what about him Tranio?

TRANIO:
If he looks believable and believes my story,
I'll make him happy to act the part of Vincentio;
and to give Baptista Minola the guarantee, as
though he really were Vincentio. Take your
love inside, and leave me alone. *[Bianca and
Lucentio exit as the Pedant enters]*

PEDANT:
Good day to you sir.

TRANIO:
And to you sir. You are welcome. Are you
traveling far, or are you staying here?

PEDANT:
Sir, I'm here for a week or two.

TRANIO:
Where are you from?

PEDANT:
From Mantua.

TRANIO:
From Mantua, sir? Oh dear, God forbid! And
you've come to Padua, unconcerned for your
life?

PEDANT:
My life, sir! I beg you, what do you mean?

TRANIO:
It's death for anyone from Mantua to come
to Padua. Don't you know why? The duke
has written and declared it everywhere.

PEDANT:
Oh no sir, the worse for me.

BIONDELLO:
Master, a mercatante or a pedant, I know
not what; but formal in apparel, in gait
and countenance, surely like a father.

LUCENTIO:
And what of him Tranio?

TRANIO:
If he be credulous, and trust my tale,
I'll make him glad to seem Vincentio; and
give assurance to Baptista Minola, as if
he were the right Vincentio. Take in your
love, and let me alone. *[Bianca and
Lucentio exit as the Pedant enters]*

PEDANT:
God save you sir!

TRANIO:
And you sir. You are welcome. Travel you
far on, or are you at the farthest?

PEDANT:
Sir, at the farthest for a week or two.

TRANIO:
What countryman, I pray?

PEDANT:
Of Mantua.

TRANIO:
Of Mantua, sir? Marry, God forbid! And
come to Padua, careless of your life?

PEDANT:
My life, sir! How, I pray?

TRANIO:
'Tis death for any one in Mantua to come
to Padua. Know you not the cause? The
duke hath published and proclaimed it openly.

PEDANT:
Alas sir, the worse for me.

*(Bi rises, picks up books; Luc
takes stools, exits UC as Ped
enters DR, head down reading
book, Xing DL; Tra X DC into
his path; Ped bumps into Tra;
Bio X to R of Ped)*

*(Ped looks to Bio who nods his
head)*

(turning back to Tra)

Act Four · Scene 2   **vernacular**

TRANIO:
Well sir, to do you a favor, I'll—but
first tell me, have you ever been to Pisa?

PEDANT:
Yes sir, I have often been to Pisa.

TRANIO:
Do you know one Vincentio?

PEDANT:
I don't know him, but I have heard of
him; a merchant of incomparable wealth.

TRANIO:
He is my father sir; and truly, in looks
rather resembles you.

BIONDELLO: *[aside]*
As much as an apple does an oyster!

TRANIO:
To save your life, I'll do you this favor,
you shall take on his name and reputation,
and you'll live at my house till you have
finished your business in this city. If
this seems like a kindness sir, just accept it.

PEDANT:
Oh sir, I do; and I will always think of you
as the protector of my life and liberty.

TRANIO:
Then come with me to arrange things. My
father is expected any day, to guarantee
the prenuptial agreement between me and
a Signior Baptista's daughter. I'll fill
you in on all the details. Come with me
sir. *[they exit]*

TRANIO:
Well sir, to do you courtesy, this will I
do—first, tell me, have you ever been at Pisa?

PEDANT:
Ay sir, in Pisa have I often been.

TRANIO:
Know you one Vincentio?

PEDANT:
I know him not, but I have heard of him;
a merchant of incomparable wealth.

TRANIO:
He is my father sir; and, sooth to say,
in countenance somewhat doth resemble you.

BIONDELLO: *[aside]*
As much as an apple does an oyster!

TRANIO:
To save your life, this favor will I do,
his name and credit shall you undertake,
and in my house you shall be friendly
lodged till you have done your business in
the city. If this be courtesy sir, accept it.

PEDANT:
Oh sir, I do; and will repute you ever
the patron of my life and liberty.

TRANIO:
Then go with me to make the matter good.   *(as Bio & Tra escort Ped DL,*
My father is here looked for every day,   *Tra hastily fills in these*
to pass assurance of a dower in marriage   *final "details")*
'twixt me and one Baptista's daughter. In
all these circumstances I'll instruct you.
Go with me sir. *[they exit]*   *(exits DL)*

Act Four · Scene 3   scene description

We now switch back to Petruchio's house in Verona. Kate is famished and exhausted and is begging Grumio to bring her some food. He tempts her with various dishes, then finds an excuse not to bring them to her.

On comes Petruchio with a plate of food which he refuses to give to Kate until she thanks him for it. She finally does so and just as she has begun to eat, Petruchio distracts her with the entrance of the tailor who has new clothing for Kate.

The food is removed, and Petruchio proceeds to present Kate with a pretty new hat and gown, which he then promptly takes away from her. Petruchio tells Kate that they will take a trip to her father's house dressed as they are and makes the point that it is what is inside of a person that counts and not what they are wearing.

Petruchio then states that it is seven o'clock, and when Kate tries to correct him and tell him that it is actually two, he says the trip is off.

Act Four · Scene 3   vernacular

[enter Katherina and Grumio]

GRUMIO:
No, no, on my life I don't dare.

KATHERINA:
What, did he marry me just to famish me?
I'm starved for food, dizzy from lack
of sleep; I'm kept awake with swearing,
and with brawling, I'm fed. And what
vexes me more than any of this, he does
it all in the name of love; it's as though
if I sleep or eat, it would make me
instantly sick or immediately kill me.
Please, go and get me something to eat;
I don't care what, as long as it's food.

GRUMIO:
What do you say to a calf's-foot?

KATHERINA:
Sounds very good; please let me have it.

GRUMIO:
I'm afraid it's too spicy a dish. What
do you say to a fat tripe, well-broiled?

KATE:
It's just fine; good Grumio, bring it to me.

GRUMIO:
I'm not sure, it's too rich. What do you
say to a piece of beef with mustard.

KATHERINA:
That's a dish that I love to eat.

GRUMIO:
Yep, but the mustard is a little too hot.

KATHERINA:
Why then the beef and forget the mustard.

GRUMIO:
No way, I will not; you shall have the
mustard or you don't get any beef from Grumio.

(Gru runs on from SR with K following; as he speaks he X to ladder, reveals "Pet House" sign as K ends up on floor DC)

[enter Katherina and Grumio]
GRUMIO:
No, no, I dare not for my life.

KATHERINA:
What, did he marry me to famish me? I'm starved for meat, giddy for lack of sleep; with oaths kept waking and with brawling fed. And, that which spites me more than all these wants, he does it under name of perfect love; as who should say, if I should sleep or eat, 'twere deadly sickness or else present death. I prithee, go and get me some repast; I care not what, so it be wholesome food.

GRUMIO:
What say you to a neat's foot?

(Xing to L of K)

KATHERINA:
'Tis passing good; I prithee let me have it.

(Gru starts off SR, stops, comes back to R of K)

GRUMIO:
I fear it is too choleric a meat. How say you to a fat tripe, finely broiled?

KATHERINA:
I like it well; good Grumio, fetch it me.

(Gru starts off SR again, stops, comes back to R of K)

GRUMIO:
I cannot tell, I fear 'tis choleric. What say you to a piece of beef and mustard.

KATHERINA:
A dish that I do love to feed upon.

(starts off again, comes back again)

GRUMIO:
Ay, but the mustard is too hot a little.

KATHERINA:
Why then the beef and let the mustard rest.

GRUMIO:
Nay then, I will not; you shall have the mustard or else you get no beef of Grumio.

(raising himself to his full height)

Act Four · Scene 3   **vernacular**

KATHERINA:
Then both, or one, or whatever you bring.

GRUMIO:
How 'bout the mustard without the beef?

KATHERINA:
Go, get out, you lying deceitful wretch.
Grief come to you–the whole lot of you,
who are reveling in my misery!

PETRUCHIO: *[enters with plate of food]*
How is my Kate? What darling, are you
depressed? Be happy, look cheerful. Here
my love; you see how diligent I am, to
carve your meat myself and bring it to
you. I am sure, sweet Kate, kindness like
this deserves thanks. What, not a word?
I see then, you don't like it and all
my trouble has been for nothing.
Here, take away this dish.

KATHERINA:
Please, let it stay.

PETRUCHIO:
Even a simple gesture should be repaid
with thanks; and so shall mine before
you touch this food.

KATHERINA:
I thank you sir.

PETRUCHIO:
May it do your sweet self good! Kate,
eat it up. And now, my dear love, we will
return to your father's house. *[Grumio
brings on tailor]* The tailor waits on
you to dress you in a gown, brand new.
What, have you finished? Come on tailor,
let's see these adornments.

TAILOR:
Here is the cap your worship ordered.

| Act Four • Scene 3 **original abridged** | Act Four • Scene 3   **stage directions** |

KATHERINA:
Then both, or one, or anything thou wilt.

GRUMIO:
Why then, the mustard without the beef!

(with a great big grin)

KATHERINA:
Go, get thee gone, thou false deluding
slave. Sorrow on thee and all the pack
of you, that triumph thus upon my misery!

(K raises herself up a bit and yells threateningly at Gru; he runs SR as Pet enters SR with plate of meat in his R hand; Gru gives Pet the "thumbs up" sign; Pet X to R of K, kneels on one knee, shows K plate of food; she reaches for it, he pulls it away)

PETRUCHIO: *[enters with plate of food]*
How fares my Kate? What, sweeting, all
amort? Pluck up thy spirits, look
cheerfully upon me. Here love; thou seest
how diligent I am, to dress thy meat
myself and bring it thee. I am sure, sweet
Kate, this kindness merits thanks. What,
not a word? Nay then, thou lov'st it not,
and all my pains is sorted to no proof.
Here, take away this dish.

(she stares defiantly at him)

(Pet turns to Gru)

KATHERINA:
I pray you, let is stand.

(as Gru starts in to get plate, K speaks; Gru stops)

PETRUCHIO:
The poorest service is repaid with thanks;
and so shall mine, before you touch the
meat.

(Pet looks at K, waiting)

KATHERINA:
I thank you sir.

(she finally speaks)

PETRUCHIO:
Much good do it unto thy gentle heart!
Kate eat apace. Now, my honey love, will
we return unto thy father's house. *[Grumio
brings on tailor]* The tailor stays your
leisure to deck thy body with his ruffling
treasure. What, hast thou dined? Come
tailor, let us see these ornaments.

(Pet hands her plate, then nods to Gru who exits SL, brings Tailor on to DLC; Tailor has cap & gown, K, who has been eatting food, rises, X to Tailor; Pet picks up plate hands it to Gru then X to L of Tailor; Gru takes plate off SR then comes DR of ladder)

TAILOR:
Here is the cap your worship did bespeak.

(holding up cap)

Act Four · Scene 3   **vernacular**

PETRUCHIO:
Why this is a knick-knack, a bauble, an
oddity, a baby's cap; take it away, and
let me have a bigger one.

KATHERINA:
I don't want one bigger; this is what's
in fashion, and gentlewomen wear caps
like these.

PETRUCHIO:
When you are gentle, you shall have one
too, but not till then. Your gown. Come
on tailor, let's see it. Oh mercy, God!
What's this? A sleeve? It's looks like
a cannon. All up and down, carved up like
an apple tart? Why, what in the devil's
name tailor, do you call this?

TAILOR:
You told me to make it according to the
fashion of the time.

PETRUCHIO:
So I did; but if you recall, I did not
ask you to mangle it at anytime. I'll
have no part of it; take it away.

KATHERINA:
I never saw a better designed gown, more
elegant, more pleasing, nor more
praiseworthy. *[to Petruchio]* It seems
you want to turn me into a puppet.

PETRUCHIO:
True; he means to turn you into a puppet.

TAILOR:
She says, your worship means to turn her
into a puppet.

PETRUCHIO:
Oh, monstrous arrogance! You flea, you
nit! Threatened in my own house! Away
you rag! I tell you truly, that you have
ruined her gown.

|

PETRUCHIO:
Why 'tis a knack, a toy, a trick, a baby's cap; away with it, let me have a bigger.

(Pet takes cap, looks at it; as he hands it back to Tailor, K reaches for it; she & Pet have "tug-of-war" with cap across Tailor)

KATHERINA:
I'll have no bigger; this doth fit the time, and gentlewomen wear such caps as these.

PETRUCHIO:
When you are gentle, you shall have one too, and not till then. Thy gown. Come tailor, let us see it. Oh mercy, God! What's this? A sleeve? 'Tis like a cannon. What, up and down, carved like an apple tart? Why, what a' devil's name, tailor, call thou this?

(Pet yanks hard; K lets go; Pet tosses hat offstage L; Tailor holds up gown; Pet takes sleeve & holds it out)

TAILOR:
You bid me make it according to the fashion and the time.

PETRUCHIO:
Marry, and did; but if you be remembered, I did not bid you mar it to the time. I'll none of it; hence.

(flips sleeve back toward Tailor)

KATHERINA:
I never saw a better fashioned gown, more quaint, more pleasing, nor more commendable. [to Petruchio] Belike you mean to make a puppet of me.

(talking across Tailor who watches intently)

PETRUCHIO:
Why true; he means to make a puppet of thee.

(speaking to K, pointing at Tailor who is cringing)

TAILOR:
She says, your worship means to make a puppet of her.

(sheepishly to Pet)

PETRUCHIO:
Oh, monstrous arrogance! Thou flea, thou nit! Braved in mine own house! Away thou rag! I tell thee, I, that thou hast marred her gown.

(furious, turning on Tailor)

(Tailor drops gown, nearly trips over it as he scurries DS &

TAILOR:
Your worship's misled; the gown was made
just as my master was directed: Grumio
placed the order.

GRUMIO:
I didn't give him any order; I just-gave
him the stuff.

TAILOR:
But how did you desire to have it made?

GRUMIO:
Really sir, with needle and thread!

PETRUCHIO:
Briefly sir, the gown is not for me.

GRUMIO:
You're right sir; it's for my mistress.

PETRUCHIO: *[to Tailor]*
Go, take it up for your master's use.

GRUMIO:
Villain, not on your life! Take up my
mistress' gown for your master's use!

PETRUCHIO:
Why sir, what do you mean by that?

GRUMIO:
Oh sir, the meaning is more profound than
you think—take up my mistress' gown
for his master's use! Oh, fie, fie, fie!

PETRUCHIO: *[aside to Grumio]*
See that the tailor is paid. *[aloud]* Go,
take it away; go! *[Tailor exits]* Well,
come on my Kate; we will go to your
father's even in these respectable, humble
clothes. For it is the mind that enriches
the body; and even as the sun breaks
through the darkest clouds, so honor shows
through the simplest of garb. What, is
the jay more precious than the lark,

Act Four · Scene 3 **original abridged**

Act Four · Scene 3 **stage directions**

TAILOR:
Your worship is deceived; the gown is made just as my master had direction: Grumio gave order how it should be done.

around behind K for protection)

GRUMIO:
I gave him no order; I gave him the stuff.

(Xing DS to between Pet & K)

TAILOR:
But how did you desire it should be made?

(peeking out from behind K)

GRUMIO:
Marry sir, with needle and thread!

PETRUCHIO:
Well sir, in brief, the gown is not for me.

GRUMIO:
You are in the right sir; 'tis for my mistress.

PETRUCHIO: *[to Tailor]*
Go, take it up unto thy master's use.

(Pet kicks gown; Tailor picks it up holding it in front of him by the shoulders)

GRUMIO:
Villain, not for thy life! Take up my mistress' gown for thy master's use!

(Gru X to L of Tailor; K counters US a little)

PETRUCHIO:
Why sir, what's your conceit in that?

(Xing L of Gru)

GRUMIO:
Oh sir, the conceit is deeper than you think—take up my mistress' gown to his master's use! Oh, fie, fie, fie!

(lifting up the skirt of the gown to demonstate his meaning)

PETRUCHIO: *[aside to Grumio]*
See the tailor paid. *[aloud]* Go, take it hence; begone! *[Tailor exits]* Well, come my Kate; we will unto your father's even in these honest mean habiliments. For 'tis the mind that makes the body rich; and as the sun breaks through the darkest clouds, so honor peereth in the meanest habit. What, is the jay more precious than the lark because his feathers are more beauti-

(whispering to Gru; Gru then escorts the Tailor DS & around to SL exit; Tailor scurries off; Gru stands SL; K kneels weeping; Pet X to K, kneels to her; this speech should to delivered with great honesty and tenderness)

because his feathers are more beautiful?
Or is the adder better than the eel,
because his skin is more colorful? Oh
no, good Kate; and neither are you any
the worse because of these paltry
furnishings and humble clothes. Then be
happy; we will leave immediately, to feast
and enjoy ourselves at your father's house.
Let's see, I think it's now seven o'clock,
and we'll easily get there by dinner time.

KATHERINA:
I assure you sir, it's almost two, and
it will be supper time before you get there.

PETRUCHIO:
It shall be seven before I get on my horse.
Look, what I speak, or do, or think to
do, you are still contradicting it. I
won't go today; and before I do, it shall
be whatever time I say it is. *[exits]*

GRUMIO: *[aside]*
Oh boy! This rooster will raise the sun!
[exit]

Act Four • Scene 4   **scene description**

This scene takes place in front of Baptista's
house with Tranio telling the Pedant to remember
that he must act like a proper father. Baptista and
Lucentio/Cambio come out, and Tranio introduces
Baptista to his *father.* The Pedant plays his part
and gives Baptista the assurance he has been waiting
for.

Tranio then suggests that they all go to his lodging to sign the official agreement. Tranio further suggests that Baptista send Lucentio/Cambio to fetch
Bianca and to inform her that she is to be married.

Biondello, who has remained behind with
Lucentio, tries to fill his somewhat slow master in on
the plan that he should fetch Bianca and elope with
her to Saint Luke's church where there is a priest
ready and willing to marry them. Lucentio finally
picks up on the plan and goes off.

[enter Tranio and the Pedant]
TRANIO:
Sir, this is the house. Play your part
with the seriousness that fathers have.

PEDANT:
I assure you I will. But sir, here comes
your boy. *[Biondello enters]*

TRANIO:
Good fellow Biondello, did you do that
errand to Baptista?

BIONDELLO:
I told him that your father was here in Padua.

Act Four·Scene 3 original abridged

	Act Four·Scene 3 stage directions

ful? Or is the adder better than the eel because his painted skin contents the eye? Oh no good Kate; neither art thou the worse for this poor furniture and mean array. Therefore frolic; we will hence forthwith, to feast and sport us at thy father's house. Let's see, I think 'tis now some seven o'clock, and well we may come there by dinner time.

(K looks at him; they are about to kiss when Pet breaks the moment, rises, X DRC looking out)

KATHERINA:
I dare assure you sir, 'tis almost two, and 'twill be supper time ere you come there.

(rising & Xing to Pet)

PETRUCHIO:
It shall be seven ere I go to horse. Look, what I speak, or do, or think to do, you are still crossing it. I will not go today; and ere I do, it shall be what o'clock I say it is. *[exits]*

(turning to K)

(Pet strides off SR; bewildered, K follows after)

GRUMIO: *[aside]*
Why so! This gallant will command the sun! *[exit]*

(Gru X to ladder, reveals "Town Square" sign, exits SR)

Act Four·Scene 4 original abridged

Act Four·Scene 4   stage directions

[enter Tranio and the Pedant]
TRANIO:
Sir, this is the house. Hold your own with such austerity as 'longeth to a father.

(Tra enters DL; Ped follows; they X R of C; as they speak, Tra indicates house UC)

PEDANT:
I warrant you. But sir, here comes your boy. *[Biondello enters]*

(Bio enters UC, takes ladder UR, places it with sign facing audience)

TRANIO:
Sirrah Biondello, hast thou done thy errand to Baptista?

BIONDELLO:
I told him that your father was in Padua.

(X to R of Tra)

TRANIO: *[to Biondello]*
You're a good man. *[to Pedant]* Here comes
Baptista. Get ready sir. *[enter Baptista
and Lucentio]* Signior Baptista, good to
see you. *[to the Pedant]* Sir, this is
the gentleman I told you of.

PEDANT: *[to Baptista]*
Sir, my son Lucentio acquainted me with
the momentous matter of love between your
daughter and himself. I am happy to have
him married. And, if you're happy, you
shall find me ready and willing with my
consent.

BAPTISTA:
Sir, I like the simplicity and the
shortness of your reply. Therefore, if
you will guarantee my daughter a sufficient
dower, they're engaged. Your son shall
have my daughter with my consent.

TRANIO:
I thank you sir. Then, if it's all right
with you, we'll tend to the business
details at my house. Send for your daughter
by your servant, *[indicating Lucentio]*
my boy *[indicating Biondello]* shall go
and fetch the notary.

BAPTISTA:
This pleases me. Cambio, hurry on home,
and tell Bianca to get ready quickly;
and tell her that she's likely to be
Lucentio's wife!

LUCENTIO:
I pray to the gods that she will, with
all my heart!

TRANIO:
Quit wasting time with the gods, and get
going! Signior Baptista, shall I lead
the way?

TRANIO: *[to Biondello]*
Thou'rt a tall fellow. *[to Pedant]* Here
comes Baptista. Set your countenance sir.
[enter Baptista and Lucentio] Signior
Baptista, happily met. *[to the Pedant]*
Sir, this is the gentleman I told you of.

*(whispering to Ped as Bap
enters UC Xing L of C; Luc
follows, stopping DL of Bap)*

PEDANT: *[to Baptista]*
Sir, my son Lucentio made me acquainted
with a weighty cause of love between
your daughter and himself. I am content
to have him matched. And, if you please,
me shall you find ready and willing with
consent.

BAPTISTA:
Sir, your plainness and your shortness
please me well. Therefore, if you will
pass my daughter a sufficient dower, the
match is made. Your son shall have my
daughter with consent.

TRANIO:
I thank you sir. Then at my lodging, and it
I like you, we'll pass the business. Send
for your daughter by your servant here,
[indicating Lucentio] my boy *[indicating
Biondello]* shall fetch the scrivener presently.

*(Ped counters R as Tra X to
Bap to shake his hand)*
*(Tra X between Bap & Luc, winks
at Luc)*

BAPTISTA:
It likes me well. Cambio, hie you home,
and bid Bianca make her ready straight;
and tell how she's like to be Lucentio's
wife!

LUCENTIO:
I pray the gods she may, with all my
heart!

TRANIO:
Dally not with the gods, but get thee
gone! Signior Baptista, shall I lead the
way?

*(whispering to Luc then turning
back to Bap)*

Act Four • Scene 4   **vernacular**

BAPTISTA:
I follow you. *[exit Tranio, Baptista, and the Pedant]*

BIONDELLO:
Cambio.

LUCENTIO:
What, Biondello?

BIONDELLO:
You saw my master wink at you?

LUCENTIO:
What about it, Biondello?

BIONDELLO:
Baptista is safely talking with the pretend father of the pretend son.

LUCENTIO:
What of him?

BIONDELLO:
You are supposed to bring his daughter.

LUCENTIO:
And then?

BIONDELLO:
The old priest at Saint Luke's church is at your command.

LUCENTIO:
What of all this?

BIONDELLO:
I don't know—except that they're all busy. If this isn't what you were hoping for, I have no more to say, bye.

LUCENTIO:
Biondello?

BIONDELLO:
I can't stay sir, and so adieu sir. My master has told me to go to Saint Luke's

Act Four·Scene 4 **original abridged**	Act Four·Scene 4 **stage directions**

BAPTISTA:
I follow you. *[exit Tranio, Baptista and the Pedant]*

(Tra leads off DL with Bap & Ped following)

BIONDELLO:
Cambio.

(Xing to Luc)

LUCENTIO:
What say'st thou, Biondello?

BIONDELLO:
You saw my master wink upon you?

LUCENTIO:
Biondello, what of that?

BIONDELLO:
Baptista is safe talking with the deceiving father of a deceitful son.

LUCENTIO:
And what of him?

BIONDELLO:
His daughter is to be brought by you.

LUCENTIO:
And then?

BIONDELLO:
The old priest at Saint Luke's church is at your command.

LUCENTIO:
And what of all this?

BIONDELLO:
I cannot tell—except they are busied. If this be not that you look for, I have no more to say, farewell.

(starts off DL)

LUCENTIO:
Biondello?

BIONDELLO:
I cannot tarry sir, and so adieu sir. My master hath appointed me to go to Saint

(turns back to Luc)

Act Four • Scene 4   vernacular

to tell the priest to get ready. Come
with your appendage. *[exit]*

LUCENTIO: *[suddenly catching on]*
Oh!!! I may—and will! *[exit]*

Act Four • Scene 5 scene description

We are now on the road with Kate, Petruchio,
and Grumio. Petruchio has stopped to admire the
moon, and Kate points out that it is actually the
sun. Petruchio insists that it must be whatever he
calls it before they continue on their journey and
says that Kate is "crossing" him. Grumio urges Kate
to comply, and somewhat reluctantly, Kate does so,
saying that whatever Petruchio wishes to call it, she
will agree.

Petruchio then tests her and calls it the moon—
she concurs. He then says she lies and that it is actually the sun. In a remarkable moment of
awakening, Kate begins to understand that it truly
does not matter—appearances are unimportant and
that it is the heart of things that counts.

They begin onward and immediately run into
an elderly gentleman who Petruchio greets as "gentle mistress" and asks Kate to greet *her.* We now
see Kate shine, as she not only joins Petruchio in his
game, but outplays him brilliantly. She adroitly follows Petruchio's every lead and creates an opportunity to bring the sun/moon image back into the
picture in such a way that Petruchio is truly impressed.

We discover that this gentleman is the real
Vincentio and that he is on his way to visit his son
Lucentio in Padua. We note too that when
Petruchio refers next to Kate, he calls her a "gentle-
woman." Things have begun to change!

Act Four • Scene 5   vernacular

[enter Petruchio, Katherina and Grumio]
PETRUCHIO:
Come on; once more to our father's house.
Good Lord, how bright and fine shines
the moon!

KATHERINA:
The moon! The sun! It's not moonlight now.

PETRUCHIO:
I say it is the moon that shines so bright.

KATHERINA:
I know it is the sun that shines so bright.

PETRUCHIO:
Now, by my mother's son, and that's me,
it shall be moon or star or what I like,
before I travel to your father's house.
[to Grumio] Go on, back again. Evermore
crossed and crossed; nothing but crossed!

GRUMIO: *[to Katherina]*
Say what he says or we'll never go.

KATHERINA:
Go on, please, since we have come this
far, and let it be the moon or the sun
or whatever you like—and if it makes
you happy to call it a candle, from now
on I swear that's what it will be for me.

PETRUCHIO:
I say it is the moon.

Act Four · Scene 4 original abridged

Luke's, to bid the priest be ready. Come
with your appendix. *[exit]*

LUCENTIO: *[suddenly catching on]*
Oh!!! I may—and will! *[exit]*

Act Four · Scene 5 original abridged

[enter Petruchio, Katherina and Grumio]
PETRUCHIO:
Come on; once more toward our father's.
Good Lord, how bright and goodly shines
the moon!

KATHERINA:
The moon! The sun! It is not moonlight now.

PETRUCHIO:
I say it is the moon that shines so bright.

KATHERINA:
I know it is the sun that shines so bright.

PETRUCHIO:
Now, by my mother's son, and that's myself,
it shall be moon or star or what I list,
or ere I journey to your father's house.
[to Grumio] Go on, back again. Evermore
crossed and crossed; nothing but crossed!

GRUMIO: *[to Katherina]*
Say as he says or we shall never go.

KATHERINA:
Forward, I pray, since we have come so far,
and be it moon or sun or what you please—
and if you please to call it a candle,
henceforth I vow it shall be so for me.

PETRUCHIO:
I say it is the moon.

Act Four · Scene 4 stage directions

(exits DL)

(exits UC)

Act Four · Scene 5 stage directions

*(Pet & K enter UR; Pet stops
C with K to see "moon"; Gru
follows on, stops at ladder
to reveal "On The Road" sign)*

Act Four · Scene 5   **vernacular**

KATHERINA:
I know it is the moon.

PETRUCHIO:
Uh uh, then you lie; it is the blessed sun.

KATHERINA:
Then God—be blessed—it is the blessed
sun! But it's not the sun, when you say
it's not; and the moon changes with your
mind. Whatever you want it named, that
it is; and so it shall be so for Katherine.

PETRUCHIO:
Well, go on, go on! But wait! Someone's
coming. *[Vincentio enters, Petruchio
addresses him]* Good morning gentle
mistress; where are you off to? Tell me
sweet Kate, and tell me truly, have you
ever beheld a healthier looking gentlewoman? What a wonderful blush upon her
cheeks! Fair lovely maiden, again good
day to you. Sweet Kate, welcome her for
the sake of her beauty.

KATHERINA: *[to Vincentio]*
Young, blossoming virgin, pretty and
youthful and sweet, where are you off
to? Happy is the man whom the auspicious
stars have decreed you to be his bride!

PETRUCHIO:
Why what's this, Kate? I hope you're not
going mad. This is a man, old, wrinkled,
withered and not a maiden as you say he is.

KATHERINA: *[not missing a beat]*
Pardon me, old father, for my mistaking
eyes, that have been so dazzled by the sun?...
that now I see things in a brand new light!
Now I see you are a venerable father;
pardon me please, for my silly mistake.

PETRUCHIO:
Do, and tell which way you are traveling.

| Act Four • Scene 5 **original abridged** | Act Four • Scene 5 **stage directions** |

KATHERINA:
I know it is the moon.

PETRUCHIO:
Nay, then you lie; it is the blessed sun.

KATHERINA:
Then God—be blessed—it is the blessed
sun! But sun it is not, when you say it
is not; and the moon changes even as your
mind. What you will have it named, even
that it is; and so it shall be so for Katherine.

*(begins as though she is about
to utter a curse, but between
"God" & "be blessed," K gets
it!)*

PETRUCHIO:
Well, forward, forward! But soft! Company
is coming here. *[Vincentio enters,
Petruchio addresses him]* Good morrow,
gentle mistress; where away? Tell me
sweet Kate, and tell me truly too,
hast thou beheld a fresher gentlewoman?
Such war of white and red within her
cheeks! Fair lovely maid, once more
good day to thee. Sweet Kate, embrace
her for her beauty's sake.

*(Pet is very pleased and relieved;
Vin enters DR heading DL; when
Pet says "gentle mistress,"
K gives Pet a knowing look
& smiles; as Vin X past DC,
Pet & K X DS so Pet is R of
Vin, K is R of Pet; Vin turns
to them)*

KATHERINA: *[to Vincentio]*
Young budding virgin, fair and fresh and
sweet, whither away? Happy the man, whom
favorable stars allots thee for his lovely
bedfellow!

*(K X to Vin; Pet counters to
R of K)*

PETRUCHIO:
Why how now, Kate? I hope thou art not mad.
This is a man—old, wrinkled, withered—
and not a maiden, as thou say'st he is.

KATHERINA: *[not missing a beat]*
Pardon, old father, my mistaking eyes,
that have been so bedazzled with the sun?...
that everything I look on seemeth green!
Now I perceive thou art a reverend father;
pardon, I pray thee, for my mad mistaking.

*(After word "sun?," K looks at Pet with an
ironic smile; he nods, acknowledging
her triumph; they smile broadly
at each other, then K turns back to Vin &
continues)*

PETRUCHIO:
Do, and make known which way thou
travellest.

Act Four · Scene 5   vernacular

VINCENTIO:
My name is Vincentio and I am on my way
to Padua to visit a son of mine.

PETRUCHIO:
What is his name?

VINCENTIO:
Lucentio.

PETRUCHIO:
Happy to meet you! By now, your son has
married the sister of this gentlewoman,
my wife. Let me embrace old Vincentio;
and let's journey together to visit your good son
who will be delighted by your arrival.

VINCENTIO:
Is all this true?

PETRUCHIO:
Come on, let's go and see the truth of it! *[exit]*

Act Five · Scene 1   scene description

We are back in Padua and Lucentio and Bianca are eloping just as Kate, Petruchio, Vincentio, and Grumio arrive at "Lucentio's" lodgings. The Pedant answers the knock, and when he is told that the gentleman at the door is Lucentio's father, he calls him a liar and says that he himself is Lucentio's father.

At this moment Biondello returns from the church, and, having seen Lucentio and Bianca married and recognizing the real Vincentio, tries to sneak off. Vincentio sees him, and when Biondello pretends he doesn't know him, Vincentio starts to beat him. In comes Tranio and attempts to bluster his way out of the situation saying that Vincentio is a madman.

The distraught Vincentio concludes that Tranio must have murdered Lucentio and calls for his arrest. Lucentio and Bianca appear, kneel to their respective fathers, tell them that they are married,

Act Five · Scene 1   vernacular

[Gremio, Biondello, Lucentio and Bianca enter]
BIONDELLO:
Quickly and quietly sir; the priest is ready.

LUCENTIO:
I'm gone Biondello.

[Lucentio, Bianca and Biondello exit while Petruchio, Katherina, Grumio and Vincentio enter]
PETRUCHIO:
Sir, here's the door, this is Lucentio's house. *[Vincentio knocks]*

GREMIO:
They're busy in there, you'd better knock louder.

Act Four · Scene 5   original abridged

VINCENTIO:
My name is Vincentio and bound I am to
Padua to visit a son of mine.

PETRUCHIO:
What is his name?

VINCENTIO:
Lucentio.

PETRUCHIO:
Happily met! The sister to my wife, this
gentlewoman, thy son by this hath married.
Let me embrace with old Vincentio; and
wander we to see thy honest son who will
of thy arrival be full joyous.

VINCENTIO:
But is this true?

PETRUCHIO:
Come, go along and see the truth! *[exit]*

Act Four · Scene 5   stage directions

*(Pet embraces Vin as K counters
R)*

*(all exit DL; Gru follows; they
continue around to UL for their
next entrance)*

Act Five · Scene 1   original abridged

*[Gremio, Biondello, Lucentio and Bianca
enter]*
Biondello:
Softly and swiftly sir; the priest is ready.

LUCENTIO:
I fly Biondello.

*[Lucentio, Bianca and Biondello exit and
Petruchio, Katherina, Grumio and Vincentio
enter]*
PETRUCHIO:
Sir, here's the door, this is Lucentio's
house. *[Vincentio knocks]*

GREMIO:
They're busy within, you were best knock
louder.

Act Five · Scene 1   stage directions

*(Gre enters SR, reveals "Luc House"
sign, turns ladder diagonally
so rungs face UR entrance,
"peeks" DS of ladder to "spy";
then, as Gre "peeks" US of
ladder, Bio leads Bi & Luc,
his disguise removed, swiftly
from DR to exit DL; Gre never
sees them & X to DS of ladder
to "spy" more as Pet, Vin, &
K enter UL, followed by Gru;
they all X to ladder)*

(knocks at door)

(coming into view)

Act Five · Scene 1   scene description

Cont.

and beg forgiveness for their deception.

The real Vincentio now gives Baptista his assurance, and all exit leaving Kate, Petruchio, and Grumio in the street. Kate suggests they follow and see how everything turns out. Petruchio asks Kate to give him a kiss.

We now see a shy and embarrassed Kate, reluctant to kiss. Petruchio, deflated by her response, turns to Grumio and says, "Why then, let's home again." Kate then gives Petruchio a loving kiss. He is delighted. They have finally come together and are on the same team!

Act Five · Scene 1   vernacular

PEDANT: *[enters]*
Who's there knocking as though he would beat down the gate?

VINCENTIO:
Is Signior Lucentio in there sir?

PEDANT:
He's in here sir, but can't be bothered.

PETRUCHIO:
Listen sir. Please tell Signior Lucentio that his father has come from Pisa and is here at the door to speak with him.

PEDANT:
You lie; his father has come from Pisa and is here looking out the window.

VINCENTIO:
Are you his father?

PEDANT:
Yes sir; that's what his mother says, if I can believe her.

PETRUCHIO: *[to Vincentio]*
Why what's this, sir! It's downright criminal to impersonate another man.

PEDANT:
Arrest the villain.

BIONDELLO: *[reentering]*
I have witnessed the marriage, God bless 'em! But who's here? My old master, Vincentio! Now we're ruined.

VINCENTIO: *[to Biondello]*
Come here, you rascal; what, have you forgotten me?

BIONDELLO:
Forgotten you? No sir. I couldn't forget

Act Five·Scene 1 **original abridged**	Act Five·Scene 1 **stage directions**

PEDANT: *[enters]*
What's he that knocks as he would beat down the gate?

(climbs up ladder from UR, stands at top, looking down at them; he is sloshed*)

VINCENTIO:
Is Signior Lucentio within sir?

(looking up at Ped)

PEDANT:
He's within sir, but not to be spoken withal.

PETRUCHIO:
Do you hear, sir? I pray you, tell Signior Lucentio that his father is come from Pisa and is here at the door to speak with him.

PEDANT:
Thou liest; his father is come from Pisa, and here looking out the window.

VINCENTIO:
Art thou his father?

PEDANT:
Ay sir; so his mother says, if I may believe her.

PETRUCHIO: *[to Vincentio]*
Why how now, gentleman! Why this is flat knavery, to take upon you another man's name.

PEDANT:
Lay hands on the villain.

BIONDELLO: *[reentering]*
I have seen them in the church together; God send 'em good shipping! But who is here? Mine old master, Vincentio! Now we are undone.

(all look up at Ped while Bio enters DL, talking to himself as he X toward "Luc" house; as he gets to C, he stops, recognizes Vin, starts to sneak off DL as Vin turns & sees him)

VINCENTIO: *[to Biondello]*
Come hither, you rogue; what, have you forgot me?

(Vin X to C)

BIONDELLO:
Forgot you? No, sir. I could not forget

(Xing to Vin)

you, because I never saw you before in my life!

VINCENTIO:
What, you notorious villain, haven't you ever seen your master's father, Vincentio?

BIONDELLO:
What, my old, beloved old master? Yes, of course sir; see where he's looking out the window.

VINCENTIO:
Is that so?

BIONDELLO:
Help, help, help! Here's a madman who wants to murder me.

PEDANT:
Help, son! Help, Signior Baptista! *[exits]*

PETRUCHIO:
Come on Kate, let's stand over here and see how this ends up.

[enter Pedant, Baptista and Tranio]
TRANIO:
Sir, who do you think you are to beat my servant?

VINCENTIO:
Who do I think I am, sir? No, who do you think you are, sir? Oh dear God! Oh fine villain! A silk jacket! Velvet trousers! Cloak and hat! While I stay at home, my son and my servant spend a fortune at the university.

TRANIO: *[with bravado]*
What's this? What's the matter?

BAPTISTA: *[to Tranio]*
What, is he crazy?

you, for I never saw you before in all
my life!

VINCENTIO:
What, you notorious villain, didst thou
never see thy master's father, Vincentio?

BIONDELLO:
What, my old, worshipful old master? Yes,
marry sir; see where he looks out of the
window.

VINCENTIO:
Is't so indeed?

BIONDELLO:
Help, help, help! Here's a madman will
murder me.

PEDANT:
Help, son! Help, Signior Baptista! *[exits]*

PETRUCHIO:
Prithee Kate, let's stand aside and see
the end of this controversy.

[enter Pedant, Baptista, and Tranio]
TRANIO:
Sir, what are you that beat my servant?

VINCENTIO:
What am I, sir? Nay, what are you, sir?
Oh immortal gods! Oh fine villain! A silk
doublet! Velvet hose! Cloak and hat! While
I'm at home, my son and my servant spend
all at the university.

TRANIO: *[with bravado]*
How now? What's the matter?

BAPTISTA: *[to Tranio]*
What, is the man lunatic?

(pointing up to Ped)

*(Vin grabs Bio by the shoulders
& shakes him)*

*(descending ladder as he speaks,
exits UR)*

*(Pet, K & Gru X to L of UC to
watch)*
*(enter UR, US of ladder, Tra
X to Vin; Bap & Ped stop DS
of ladder)*

*(releasing Bio, who immediately
runs off DL, Vin turns to Tra
who takes a huge, noisy intake
of breath; Vin looks Tra up
& down)*

(trying to recover his composure)

(Xing D to R of Tra)

Act Five · Scene 1   vernacular

TRANIO: *[to Vincentio]*
Sir, you're dressed like a sober old
gentleman, but you talk like a madman.
Why sir, what business is it to you what
I wear. I thank my good father *[indicating
Pedant]* that I can afford it.

VINCENTIO:
Your father? Oh you villain! He is a sail-
maker in Bergamo.

BAPTISTA:
You're mistaken sir; you're mistaken;
what do you think his name is?

VINCENTIO:
His name—as if I didn't know his name!
I have brought him up since he was three
years old, and his name is Tranio.

PEDANT:
Away, away, you mad ass! His name is
Lucentio; and he is my only son, and the
heir to me, Signior Vincentio.

VINCENTIO:
Lucentio! Oh, he has murdered his master!
Arrest him, I order you. Oh, my son, my
son! Tell me you villain, where is my
son, Lucentio?

*[reenter Biondello with Lucentio and
Bianca]*
BIONDELLO:
There he is; deny him, renounce him, or
else we're ruined. *[Biondello, Tranio
and Pedant exit]*

LUCENTIO:
Pardon me, sweet father.

VINCENTIO:
Is my sweet son alive?

BIANCA:
Pardon me, dear father.

Act Five·Scene 1   **original abridged**

Act Five·Scene 1   **stage directions**

TRANIO: *[to Vincentio]*
Sir, you seem a sober ancient gentleman
by your habit, but your words show you a
madman. Why sir, what concerns it you what
I wear? I thank my good father, *[indicating
Pedant]* I am able to maintain it.

VINCENTIO:
Thy father? Oh villain! He is a sail-maker
in Bergamo.

BAPTISTA:
You mistake sir; you mistake sir; pray
what do you think is his name?

VINCENTIO:
His name? as if I knew not his name! I
have brought him up since he was three
years old and his name is Tranio.

PEDANT:
Away, away, mad ass! His name is Lucentio;   *(from where he is, very drunk-*
and he is mine only son, and heir to the   *enly)*
lands of me, Signior Vincentio.

VINCENTIO:
Lucentio! Oh, he hath murdered his master!
Lay hold on him, I charge you. Oh, my son,
my son! Tell me thou villain, where is my
son, Lucentio?

[reenter Biondello with Lucentio and   *(Bio enters DL with Luc & Bi*
Bianca]   *following)*
BIONDELLO:
Yonder he is; deny him, forswear him, or
else we are all undone. *[Biondello, Tranio*   *(Bio runs US to exit UR; Tra*
and Pedant exit]   *& Ped follow)*

LUCENTIO:
Pardon, sweet father.   *(Luc X to Vin & kneels)*

VINCENTIO:
Lives my sweet son?

BIANCA:
Pardon, dear father.   *(Bi X to Bap & kneels)*

Act Five · Scene 1   **vernacular**

BAPTISTA:
What have you done wrong? Where is Lucentio?

LUCENTIO:
Here is Lucentio; the real son to the real Vincentio; who has by marriage made your daughter mine.

VINCENTIO:
Where is that damned villain, Tranio?

BAPTISTA:
But tell me, isn't this Cambio?

BIANCA:
Cambio is changed into Lucentio.

LUCENTIO:
Love made these miracles. Bianca's love made me trade places with Tranio. What Tranio did, he did for me; then pardon him, sweet father, for my sake.

BAPTISTA:
But sir, have you married my daughter without my consent?

VINCENTIO:
Don't worry Baptista; we'll make it good. But I'm going in to be revenged for this wickedness. *[exit]*

BAPTISTA:
And I, to get to the bottom of this deception. *[exit]*

LUCENTIO:
Don't worry, Bianca; your father will forgive us. *[they exit]*

GREMIO:
My hopes are dashed! But I'll go in too; with no hopes for anything but a good dinner. *[exit]*

Act Five·Scene 1 **original abridged**	Act Five·Scene 1 **stage directions**

BAPTISTA:
How hast thou offended? Where is Lucentio?

LUCENTIO:
Here's Lucentio; right son unto the right
Vincentio; that have by marriage made thy
daughter mine.

VINCENTIO:
Where is that damned villain, Tranio?

BAPTISTA:
Why tell me, is not this my Cambio?

BIANCA:
Cambio is changed into Lucentio.

LUCENTIO:
Love wrought these miracles. Bianca's love   *(rises X below Vin to Bi, takes*
made me exchange my state with Tranio.   *her hand & helps her rise,*
What Tranio did, myself enforced him to;   *then turns to Vin)*
then pardon him, sweet father, for my sake.

BAPTISTA:
But sir, have you married my daughter   *(says this to Luc who turns*
without asking my goodwill?   *to look at him)*

VINCENTIO:
Fear not Baptista; we will content you.
But I will in, to be revenged for this
villainy. *[exit]*   *(exits UR)*

BAPTISTA:
And I, to sound the depth of this knavery.
[exit]   *(exits UR)*

LUCENTIO:
Look not pale, Bianca; thy father will not
frown. *[they exit]*   *(exits UR)*

GREMIO:
My cake is dough! But I'll in among the
rest; out of hope of all, but my share of
the feast. *[exit]*   *(exits UR)*

Act Five · Scene 1   vernacular

KATHERINA:
Husband, let's go too to see how it all turns out.

PETRUCHIO:
First kiss me Kate, and then we will.

KATHERINA:
What, in the middle of the street?

PETRUCHIO:
Why, are you ashamed of me?

KATHERINA:
No sir; God forbid! But I am ashamed to kiss.

PETRUCHIO:
Why then, let's go home again. *[to Grumio]* Come on pal, let's go.

KATHERINA:
No, I will give you a kiss. *[she kisses him]* Now please, my love, stay.

PETRUCHIO:
Now isn't this good? Come on sweet Kate; better once than never, for it's never too late. *[they exit]*

Act Five · Scene 2   scene description

In this scene, everyone gathers at Lucentio's house to celebrate the various marriages. Petruchio immediately notes a discord between Hortensio and his Widow. The Widow says that Petruchio is merely projecting his own problems with Kate onto Hortensio's marriage.

Kate and the Widow exit to debate this issue with Bianca following. While the women are gone, the men decide to place a bet to determine whose wife is the most obedient. They arrange that each of them will send for his wife, and the man whose wife is the most obedient and comes when she is sent for will be the winner.

Act Five · Scene 2   vernacular

[enter Baptista, Vincentio, Gremio, Lucentio, Bianca, Petruchio, Katherina, Hortensio, Widow, Tranio, Biondello, Grumio]

LUCENTIO:
At last harmony reigns. My fair Bianca, welcome my father, while I welcome yours. Brother Petruchio, sister Katherina, and you Hortensio with your loving Widow, welcome to my house.

PETRUCHIO:
Padua offers nothing but kindness.

Act Five • Scene 1   original abridged

KATHERINA:
Husband, let's follow to see the end of this ado.

PETRUCHIO:
First kiss me Kate, and we will.

KATHERINA:
What, in the midst of the street?

PETRUCHIO:
What, art thou ashamed of me?

KATHERINA:
No sir; God forbid! But ashamed to kiss.

PETRUCHIO:
Why then, let's home again. *[to Grumio]* Come sirrah, let's away.

KATHERINA:
Nay, I will give thee a kiss. *[she kisses him]* Now prithee love, stay.

PETRUCHIO:
Is not this well? Come my sweet Kate; better once than never, for never too late. *[they exit]*

Act Five • Scene 1   stage directions

(taking Pet's hand & Xing R)

(Pet stops her)

(K turns to Pet)

(Pet starts to X L as K reaches out to stop him and then kisses him very lovingly & tenderly)

(they exit UR; Gru follows taking ladder offstage as he goes—if needed, Gre may assist)

Act Five • Scene 2   original abridged

[enter Baptista, Vincentio, Gremio, Lucentio, Bianca, Petruchio, Katherina, Hortensio, Widow, Tranio, Biondello, Grumio]

LUCENTIO:
At last our jarring notes agree. My fair Bianca, bid my father welcome, while I welcome thine. Brother Petruchio, sister Katherina, and thou Hortensio with thy loving Widow, welcome to my house.

PETRUCHIO:
Padua affords nothing but what is kind.

Act Five • Scene 2   stage directions

(Luc & Bi lead on Xing C, Luc R of Bi; others form semicircle R & L of them, L of Bi is Vin, K, & Pet; R of Luc is Bap, Hor, Wid, & Gre; Tra & Bio stay URC; Gru is ULC)
(Bi embraces Vin; Luc embraces Bap)

Act Five · Scene 2   scene description

Cont.

Lucentio goes first and sends for Bianca who sends back word that "she is busy and she cannot come." Hortensio then sends for his wife who flatly refuses to come. Finally Petruchio sends Grumio to get Kate. She immediately appears and graciously inquires as to what he might want. Once again the onlookers are stunned.

Petruchio sends Kate off instructing her to return with the other wives. Baptista is so impressed at the change in Kate that he gives Petruchio another twenty thousand crowns as a second dowry for this newly changed daughter.

When Kate returns, Petruchio demonstrates his and Kate's solidarity by asking her to throw her cap on the ground and then by telling the other wives what their relationships to their husbands should be.

Kate, who is now confident in her love for Petruchio and his love for her, delivers a wonderful speech about the responsibilities of marriage and the dedication one should feel to one's mate. We can see by Petruchio's response to Kate that he is proud and happy. Theirs will be a wonderful and successful marriage!

Act Five · Scene 2   vernacular

HORTENSIO:
For both of our sakes, I wish that were true.

PETRUCHIO:
On my life, Hortensio is afraid of his widow.

WIDOW: *[to Petruchio]*
He who is dizzy thinks the world is spinning round.

KATHERINA: *[to Widow]*
"He who is dizzy thinks the world is spinning round."—Please tell me what you meant by that.

WIDOW:
Since your husband is afflicted with a shrew, he judges my husband's troubles by his own! Now you know my meaning.

KATHERINA:
A very mean meaning.

WIDOW:
Right, I mean you.

PETRUCHIO:
Tell her Kate! *[Kate and Widow exit]*

HORTENSIO:
Tell her Widow!

BIANCA:
You are all welcome. *[she exits]*

BAPTISTA:
Now, my son Petruchio, I think you have the truest shrew of all.

PETRUCHIO:
Well I say no! And therefore, to prove it, let's each one of us send for his wife; and he, whose wife is the most obedient and comes immediately when he sends for her, shall win the wager that we shall propose.

Act Five•Scene 2   original abridged

HORTENSIO:
For both our sakes, I would that were true.

PETRUCHIO:
Now, for my life, Hortensio fears his
widow.

WIDOW: *[to Petruchio]*
He that is giddy thinks the world turns
round.

KATHERINA: *[to Widow]*
"He that is giddy thinks the world turns
round"—I pray you, tell me what you
meant by that.

WIDOW:
Your husband, being troubled with a shrew,
measures my husband's sorrow by his woe!
And now you know my meaning.

KATHERINA:
A very mean meaning.

WIDOW:
Right, I mean you.

PETRUCHIO:
To her Kate! *[Kate and the Widow exit]*

HORTENSIO:
To her, widow!

BIANCA:
You are welcome all. *[she exits]*

BAPTISTA:
Now, son Petruchio, I think thou hast the
veriest shrew of all.

PETRUCHIO:
Well, I say no! And therefore, for assurance, let's each one send unto his wife;
and he, whose wife is most obedient to
come at first when he doth send for her,
shall win the wager which we will propose.

Act Five•Scene 2   stage directions

(Xing C)

(Xing to Wid)

*(K & Wid start off UC; Bi &
Luc split to let them pass;
they exit UC, in silent but
animated conversation)*

(runs off following UC)

Act Five · Scene 2 **vernacular**

HORTENSIO:
Okay! What's the wager?

LUCENTIO:
Twenty crowns.

PETRUCHIO:
Twenty crowns! I'll bet that much on my hawk or hound, but twenty times as much on my wife.

LUCENTIO:
A hundred then.

HORTENSIO:
Okay.

PETRUCHIO:
A bet; it's set.

HORTENSIO:
Who shall go first?

LUCENTIO:
I will. Go Biondello, ask your mistress to come to me.

BIONDELLO:
I go. *[he exits]*

BAPTISTA: *[to Lucentio]*
Son, I'll take half your bet that Bianca comes.

LUCENTIO:
I'll cover it all myself. *[Biondello reenters]* What gives! What's the story?

BIONDELLO:
Sir, my mistress sends you word that she is busy and she cannot come.

PETRUCHIO:
What! She is busy and she can't come! Is that an answer?

Act Five · Scene 2 **original abridged**	Act Five · Scene 2 **stage directions**

HORTENSIO:
Content! What is the wager?

LUCENTIO:
Twenty crowns.

PETRUCHIO:
Twenty crowns! I'll venture so much upon
my hawk or hound, but twenty times so much
upon my wife.

LUCENTIO:
A hundred then.

HORTENSIO:
Content.

PETRUCHIO:
A match; 'tis done.

HORTENSIO:
Who shall begin?

LUCENTIO:
That will I. Go Biondello, bid your
mistress come to me.

*(Bio, on hearing his name, moves
to UC)*

BIONDELLO:
I go. *[he exits]*

(exits UC)

BAPTISTA: *[to Lucentio]*
Son, I will be your half, Bianca comes.

LUCENTIO:
I'll bear it all myself. *[Biondello re-
enters]* How now! What news?

(enters UC, stops)

BIONDELLO:
Sir, my mistress sends you word that she
is busy and she cannot come.

PETRUCHIO:
How! She is busy and she cannot come! Is
that an answer?

Act Five • Scene 2   **vernacular**

GREMIO:
Yes, and a kind one too. Pray God sir,
your wife doesn't send you one worse.

HORTENSIO:
Biondello, go and urge my wife to come
to me immediately. *[exit Biondello]*

PETRUCHIO:
Oh! Urge her! Oh, then she has to
come.

[reenter Biondello]
HORTENSIO:
Now where's my wife?

BIONDELLO:
She will not come; she says you should
go to her.

PETRUCHIO:
Worse and worse; she will not come! Oh
that's vile, intolerable, not to be endured! My man
Grumio, go to your mistress; say that I command
her to come to me. *[exit Grumio]*

[silence—Grumio then Katherina enter]
KATHERINA:
What did you want sir, that you sent for me?

PETRUCHIO:
Where is your sister and Hortensio's wife?

KATHERINA:
They sit chatting by the parlor fire.

PETRUCHIO:
Go, bring them here. *[exit Katherina]*

LUCENTIO:
This is wonderful!

HORTENSIO:
I wonder what it bodes.

| Act Five · Scene 2 **original abridged** | Act Five · Scene 2 **stage directions** |

GREMIO:
Ay, and a kind one too. Pray God sir,
your wife send you not a worse.

HORTENSIO:
Sirrah Biondello, go and entreat my wife
to come to me forthwith. *[exit Biondello]*

(exits UC)

PETRUCHIO:
Oh! Entreat her! Nay, then she must needs
come.

[reenter Biondello]

(enters UC, stops)

HORTENSIO:
Now where's my wife?

BIONDELLO:
She will not come; she bids you come to
her.

(Bio returns to his original URC position)

PETRUCHIO:
Worse and worse; she will not come! Oh
vile, intolerable, not to be endured!
Sirrah Grumio, go to your mistress; say,

(hearing his name, Gru X UC)

I command her come to me. *[exit Grumio]*

(exits UC)

[silence—Grumio then Katherina enter]

(silence as all eyes are UC;
Gru enters looking dejected,
X to ULC; suddenly K appears
UC, Xing DC to Pet)

KATHERINA:
What is your will sir, that you send for me?

PETRUCHIO:
Where is your sister and Hortensio's wife?

KATHERINA:
They sit conferring by the parlor fire.

PETRUCHIO:
Go, fetch them hither. *[exit Katherina]*

(exits UC)

LUCENTIO:
Here is a wonder!

HORTENSIO:
I wonder what it bodes.

Act Five • Scene 2   **vernacular**

PETRUCHIO:
Surely, it bodes peace, and love, and
a quiet life; and in brief, sweetness
and happiness.

BAPTISTA:
Good Petruchio, you've won the wager;
and I will add twenty thousand crowns
to what they owe, another dowry for another
daughter, she is changed into a new person.

PETRUCHIO:
And I will win that wager even more; and
show more signs of her obedience. *[enter
Katherina with Bianca and Widow]* See where
she comes and brings your disobedient
wives. Katherine, that cap of yours does
nothing for you; take it off and throw
it on the ground.

WIDOW:
Lord, let me never be brought to such
silliness!

BIANCA:
Oh! What sort of foolish duty do you call this?

LUCENTIO:
I wish your duty were as foolish. Your
"clever" duty, fair Bianca, has cost me
a hundred crowns since supper-time.

BIANCA:
You're the bigger fool for wagering on
my duty.

PETRUCHIO:
Katherine, I order you to tell these
stubborn women what duty they owe their
lords and husbands.

WIDOW:
Come on; we won't be lectured.

PETRUCHIO:
Come on, I say.

Act Five · Scene 2   **original abridged**

Act Five · Scene 2   **stage directions**

PETRUCHIO:
Marry, peace it bodes, and love, and
quiet life; and, to be short, what not
that's sweet and happy.

BAPTISTA:
Good Petruchio, the wager thou hast won;
and I will add unto their losses twenty
thousand crowns, another dowry to another
daughter, for she is changed as she had
never been.

PETRUCHIO:
Nay, I will win my wager better yet; and
show more sign of her obedience. *[enter
Katherina with Bianca and Widow]* See
where she comes and brings your froward
wives. Katherine, that cap of yours
becomes you not; off with that bauble,
throw it under foot.

*(K brings Bi & Wid on UC; K
X to Pet; Bi & Wid go to their
original positions)*

(K removes cap, throws it down)

WIDOW:
Lord, let me never be brought to such a
silly pass!

BIANCA:
Fie! What foolish duty call you this?

LUCENTIO:
I would your duty were as foolish too. The
wisdom of your duty, fair Bianca, hath cost
me a hundred crowns since supper-time.

BIANCA:
The more fool you, for laying on my duty.

(all except K & Pet say "oooh")

PETRUCHIO:
Katherine, I charge thee, tell these
headstrong women what duty they do owe
their lords and husbands.

WIDOW:
Come, come; we will have no telling.

PETRUCHIO:
Come on, I say.

Act Five·Scene 2   vernacular

WIDOW:
She shall not.

PETRUCHIO:
I say she shall; and begin with her. *[he indicates the Widow]*

KATHERINA:
Fie, fie! Ease that threatening, unkind brow; and don't cast scornful looks from your eyes, to wound your lord, your king, your governor. It ruins your beauty, and is in no way proper or friendly. Your husband is your lord, your life, your keeper, your guide, your king; one who takes care of you, and to support you, performs difficult labors, and asks for nothing in return, but your love, gentle looks and your obedience—too little payment for such a great debt. Such duty as the subject owes to his prince, even that a woman owes to her husband. I am ashamed that women are so silly to want to wrangle when they should be looking for peace; or want rule, supremacy and power, when they ought to serve, love and obey. Come, come! I was as defiant as you, my spirit as strong; my reason, perhaps even greater. But now I see...Then cease your arrogance—it's of no use, and place your hands beneath your husbands' foot. In token of that duty, if it will please, my hand is ready, may it give him ease!

PETRUCHIO:
Why, that's my girl! Come on, and kiss me Kate. *[she does so without hesitation]*

The end!

Act Five · Scene 2 **original abridged**	Act Five · Scene 2 **stage directions**

WIDOW:
She shall not.

PETRUCHIO:
I say she shall; and begin with her. *[he indicates the Widow]*

KATHERINA:
Fie, fie! Unknit that threatening, unkind brow; and dart not scornful glances from those eyes, to wound thy lord, thy king, thy governor. It blots thy beauty, and in no sense is meet or amiable. Thy husband is thy lord, thy life, thy keeper, thy head, thy sovereign; one that cares for thee, and for thy maintenance commits his body to painful labor, and craves no other tribute at thy hands, but love, fair looks and true obedience—too little payment for so great a debt. Such duty as the subject owes the prince, even such a woman oweth to her husband. I am ashamed that women are so simple to offer war, where they should kneel for peace; or seek for rule, supremacy and sway, when they are bound to serve, love, and obey. Come, come! My mind hath been as big as one of yours, my heart as great; my reason, haply more. But now I see...Then vail your stomachs, for it is no boot, and place your hands below your husband's foot. In token of which duty, if he please, my hand is ready, may it do him ease.

(Xing C, looking at Wid)

(indicating Hor)

(turning DS, K delivers this speech with simplicity & honesty)

(turning to Pet)

(holding out her R hand)

PETRUCHIO:
Why, there's a wench! Come on, and kiss me Kate. *[she does so without hesitation]*

The end!

(slowly Xing to Pet, with her hand extended as Pet X to meet her; Pet takes her hand, kisses it after word "wench"; K kisses him; all others say "aaah"; Pet & K lead off UC, all others follow)

(We have selected our punctuation based on the First Folio and Staunton's "The Plays of Shakespeare" (1858-1861). We have taken some minor liberties with Shakespeare's text to accommodate our abridged version and for this we apologize to purists, to scholars and, most of all, to Shakespeare!)

"To what end are all these words?"

A DISCUSSION OF THE LANGUAGE IN SHAKESPEARE'S PLAYS

Having read the play, let's take a little time to look at Shakespeare's language—very different from the way we speak today!

Language evolves over the course of time. Foreign influences, developments in technology, new slang, and altered usages of words all affect the way we communicate. What is perfectly clear in 1996 might be almost incomprehensible by the year 2396.

At the time that Shakespeare wrote, English was evolving at a particularly furious pace.

In 1066, England had been conquered by Frenchmen (Normans) who made French the official language of England. The upper classes spoke French, the lower classes spoke English (which was at that time a kind of German called Saxon), while all church business was conducted in Latin.

Over the course of time, a melding of these languages occurred. And along with this, came a new national identity and pride. The inhabitants of England no longer thought of themselves as *Saxons* or *Frenchmen* but as *Englishmen.*

By the time Henry V reestablished English as the official language of the land around 1400, English was evolving into a new and extremely exciting vehicle for communication. New words and new ways of saying things became the mark of a clever person.

It was into this atmosphere that Shakespeare was born. By the time Shakespeare had come along, language was not merely a tool used to get through the day, but a song to be sung, a flag to be waved, capable of expressing anything and everything. It was a kind of national sport. The basic rules had been laid down and now the sky was the limit. Everyone was a *rapper,* a *wordsmith.* And Shakespeare was better at this game than anyone of his time and perhaps since. It is said that Shakespeare added over a thousand *new* words to the language.

Getting *easy* with Shakespeare is like learning to read or drive; once you get the hang of it, your world is changed.

Language is the *guardian* at the entrance gate to the land of Shakespeare. To enter, one must *tame* the guardian. This simply means that you must take the time to become familiar with his ways.

And now for the good news, once you learn the guardian's ways, he changes. He ceases to be an obstacle and instead becomes your guide and ally; your conveyance to Shakespeare's world and mind.

Let's examine a few of the techniques that will help you to tame the guardian and make your exploration of Shakespeare easier.

1. The first thing to do is to find out what all the words mean. To do this, you will want to go to your local library and gather any Shakespeare lexicons or glossaries and as many different dictionaries and thesauri as you can locate, along with all the versions of *The Taming of the Shrew* that they have (with all their various footnotes and explanations) and look up all the words you don't know. Note their various meanings and try to determine which works best for the context you found the word in.

2. We must remember that Shakespeare, as well as other poets, took *poetic license*—poets will allow themselves to deviate from accepted form in order to achieve a desired effect. Poets will often rearrange words to achieve a more musical, poetical structure, or perhaps to get a rhyme to occur at the end of a line.

Sometimes, by merely rearranging the subject, verb, adverbs, etc. of a complicated sentence, we can more easily understand its meaning.

For example, in Act 2 scene 1, when Kate says, "No such jade as you *if me you mean,*" this can be clarified by simply turning the phrase around to read, "No such jade as you *if you mean me.*" (Note that by changing Shakespeare's language, his poetry is sacrificed, so always remember to go back to the original.)

3. Shakespeare also takes words and *stretches* their obvious meanings. He will use a word in a correct, but somewhat unusual manner so that he makes us see something in a whole new light.

When Hortensio says of Kate, "Though it pass your patience and mine to endure her..." in Act 1 scene 1, Shakespeare is having him use the word "pass" in a rather unique way.

We generally think of the word *pass* in terms of handing something off to someone else, or a *free pass* to get into a movie, or to move beyond the car in front of you on the freeway, or even to *pass* a bill in Congress, but we rarely think of it as Shakespeare uses it here. What Shakespeare has done is to take the idea of *passing* in the sense of *going beyond* and stretched its meaning to include the idea of *excessiveness.* So what Hortensio means is that it *exceeds* his patience and Gremio's to put up with Kate.

Another example of Shakespeare stretching meanings can be found in the line, "Were it not that my fellow schoolmaster doth watch Bianca's steps so narrowly..." In this case Shakespeare has used the word *narrowly* in a unique manner. We usually think of *narrow* in terms of a *narrow escape* or a not very wide passageway perhaps. Here Shakespeare is taking that idea of *not very wide* and using it in such a way as to suggest that Hortensio is watching Bianca's comings and going so very closely that there is a narrow margin between his *eyeballs* and her *footsteps!* What a wonderfully rich image.

When we come across a situation like this, we must look at the context of the unusual usage and use our imaginations to stretch the meanings of the word as Shakespeare might have done. Once we start thinking like Shakespeare, we can open ourselves to the various *shades* of meaning contained in words.

4. Shakespeare's use of the apostrophe sometimes makes words seem strange to us, but when we realize that he is using it no differently than we do in modern English, the words become easy to understand.

An apostrophe merely tells us that something is missing. For example, in the word "I'll," the apostrophe replaces "wi." "I'll" is a contraction for "I will." So with Shakespeare, the word "'tis" means "it is." Shakespeare often contracts words in this manner to alter the number of syllables in a line in order to fit his poetic structure.

5. Yet another thing to keep in mind when dealing with Shakespeare is that most of the punctuation in the versions you will read was put there by an editor in subsequent centuries and was not Shakespeare's.

Quite frankly, Shakespeare was more concerned with meaning than with grammatically correct punctuation. He was writing for actors and his objective with punctuation was to clarify how an actor should interpret a line. In fact, it is thought that many of the actors in Shakespeare's company could not read and the learning of a script was an oral process.

Therefore, a good way to get more comfortable with Shakespeare, might be to *listen* to professional actors on recordings of Shakespeare's plays and follow along in a script. Don't be afraid to imitate what you hear, it is an excellent way to learn.

6. We find though, that the very best way to become comfortable with Shakespeare and his language is to work with the material *out loud*. There is something marvelous that happens when we say the words aloud that helps to clarify their meanings.

Merely reading about baseball rarely improves your technique. So with Shakespeare, his material was meant to be *performed,* and therefore, the best way to connect to and understand the material is to speak it out loud, preferably with other people—but even alone works wonders.

You'll be amazed to discover Shakespeare's language becoming clearer and clearer as you work this way. Just remember; patience and practice!

Taming the guardian

EXERCISES TO HELP UNDERSTAND
SHAKESPEARE'S LANGUAGE

This exercise is designed to put into practice the various techniques for understanding Shakespeare that we have just talked about.

Select one of the following speeches (which are from *The Taming of the Shrew* and have either been cut or not used in their entirety in our version of the play) and *translate* the speech into vernacular American.

This is the time to go to the library and locate all those reference books that we talked about earlier and look up all the words in the speech you've chosen. You might want to do this working as a group or in pairs, sharing your ideas as you work, or you might work individually on the same speech and then compare results after.

Once you have found the various meanings of the words, and made lists of them, you can begin to select the ones that seem most appropriate for conveying the meaning of the speech. Note that you may also need to rearrange the order of words to clarify the meaning.

Now put this all together and write a vernacular version of the speech. When doing this, try to imagine the words that the character who speaks the speech in the play might use if he or she were speaking today.

Remember, there are no right or wrong ways to do this exercise. Be creative and daring. Shakespeare certainly would be if he were around today and had our version of the English language to work with!

Now that you have broken the code and the guardian is starting to seem friendlier, go back to the *original* version of your speech and read it aloud strongly keeping in mind the meanings of the words that you have now discovered. Note how much clearer Shakespeare's language has become for you and for your listeners. This is the fact that every actor knows: *the clearer the understanding of the language, the more clearly it will be conveyed.*

Note, too, how well Shakespeare says things—in such a way that pretty much sums it up. It is not only the words he chooses, but the order he has selected to put them in that creates the incredibly rich imagery that he is so famous for. It's interesting too to see how many words it can take to translate Shakespeare's succinct images into vernacular American. You could say it differently perhaps, but not better!

This is why, while it is possible to update the language with vernacular versions, it is certainly never preferable to use them for any reason other than as a tool for getting back to the original.

He is the *Master!* And now that you are learning how to tame the guardian, you will be able enter into Shakespeare's world and begin to discover the breadth and depth of his insights into human nature.

[You will note that for this exercise, we have printed Shakespeare's text in *verse form* when it appears that way in the original. We have chosen not to use the verse form in our cut version for reasons of simplicity, but now that you have become more familiar with Shakespeare and his language, it might be a good idea to get used to it. When dealing with the verse form, do not stop at the end of the line unless there is punctuation telling you to. If there is not a period or a colon, continue reading on until the thought is complete. Also, don't be thrown by the fact that each line begins with a capitalized letter, this is merely part of the *form.* Some of the following text is printed as ordinary prose; that is how Shakespeare had it in the original. He often switched back and forth depending on the effect he wished to accomplish.]

Lucentio: (Act 1 scene 1, asking Tranio for advice upon arriving in Padua)

> Tell me thy mind, for I have Pisa left
> And am to Padua come as he that leaves
> A shallow plash to plunge him in the deep
> And with satiety seeks to quench his thirst.

Hortensio: (Act 1 scene 1, talking to Gremio about how they must proceed to get Bianca back out in the dating pool)

> a word, I pray. Though the nature of our quarrel yet never brooked parle, know now, upon advice, it toucheth us both—that we may yet again have access to our fair mistress and be happy rivals in Bianca's love—to labor and effect one thing specially.

Lucentio: (Act 1 scene 1, explaining that while he never believed in love-at-first-sight, it has taken hold of him)

> O Tranio, till I found it to be true
> I never thought it possible or likely;
> But see! while idly I stood looking on,
> I found the effect of love in idleness,
> And now in plainness do confess to thee
> That art to me as secret and as dear
> As Anna to the Queen of Carthage was—
> Tranio, I burn, I pine, I perish Tranio,
> If I achieve not this young modest girl.

Grumio: (Act 1 scene 2, reinforcing Petruchio's assertion to Hortensio that he's after a woman with money)

> Nay look you sir, he tells you flatly what his mind is: why give him gold enough and marry him to a puppet or an aglet-baby or an old trot with ne'er a tooth in her head, though she have as many diseases as two and fifty horses. Why, nothing comes amiss, so money comes withal.

Baptista: (Act 2 scene 1, reprimanding Kate for being cruel to Bianca)

> Why, how now dame! Whence grows this insolence?
> Bianca, stand aside—poor girl, she weeps.
> Go, ply thy needle; meddle not with her.
> For shame, thou hilding of a devilish spirit,
> Why dost thou wrong her that did ne'er wrong thee?
> When did she cross thee with a bitter word?

Kate: (Act 2 scene 1, furious that Baptista is defending Bianca)

> What, will you not suffer me? Nay, now I see
> She is your treasure, she must have a husband;
> I must dance barefoot on her wedding-day,
> And for your love to her, lead apes in hell.
> Talk not to me! I will go sit and weep,
> Till I can find occasion for revenge.

Tranio: (Act 2 scene 1, presenting himself to Baptista as a suitor to Bianca)

> Pardon me sir, the boldness is mine own
> That, being a stranger in this city here,
> Do make myself a suitor to your daughter,
> Unto Bianca, fair and virtuous.
> Nor is your firm resolve unknown to me,
> In the preferment of the eldest sister.
> This liberty is all that I request,
> That, upon knowledge of my parentage,
> I may have welcome 'mongst the rest that woo,
> And free access and favour as the rest.

Petruchio: (Act 2 scene 1, explaining to Baptista why he won't have any trouble courting Kate)

> Why that is nothing; for I tell you father,
> I am as peremptory as she proud-minded;
> And where two raging fires meet together,
> They do consume the thing that feeds their fury.
> Though little fire grows great with little wind,
> Yet extreme gusts will blow out fire and all.
> So I to her, and so she yields to me,
> For I am rough and woo not like a babe.

Hortensio: (Act 2 scene 1, describing his first encounter with Kate as her music teacher)

> Why no, for she hath broke the lute to me.
> I did but tell her she mistook her frets,

And bowed her hand to teach her fingering,
When (with a most impatient devilish spirit)
"Frets call you these?" quoth she, "I'll fume with
  them."
And with that word she struck me on the head,
And through the instrument my pate made way,
And there I stood amazed for a while,
As on a pillory, looking through the lute,
While she did call me rascal, fidler,
And twangling Jack, with twenty such vile terms,
As had she studied to misuse me so.

Petruchio: (Act 2 scene 1, telling Baptista how passionately Kate loves him)
I tell you 'tis incredible to believe
How much she loves me: O the kindest Kate!
She hung about my neck, and kiss on kiss
She vied to fast, protesting oath on oath,
That in a twink she won me to her love.

Tranio: (Act 2 scene 1, determining that he must locate someone to impersonate Vincentio)
'Tis in my head to do my master good:
I see no reason but supposed *Lucentio*
Must get a father called supposed *Vincentio;*
And that's a wonder: fathers commonly
Do get their children; but in this case of wooing,
A child shall get a sire, if I fail not of my cunning.

Lucentio: (Act 3 scene 1, trying to get Licio to get lost so he can be alone with Bianca)
Preposterous ass! that never read so far
To know the cause why music was ordained!
Was it not to refresh the mind of man
After his studies or his usual pain?
Then give me leave to read philosophy,
And, while I pause, serve in your harmony.

Bianca: (Act 3 scene 1, taking charge of the situation with Cambio and Licio and instructing them what to do)
Why gentlemen, you do me double wrong,
To strive for that which resteth in my choice.
I am no breeching scholar in the schools;
I'll not be tied to hours nor 'pointed times,
But learn my lessons as I please myself.
And, to cut off all strife, here sit we down.
Take you your instrument, play you the whiles;
His lecture will be done ere you have tuned.

Hortensio: (Act 3 scene 1, beginning his courtship of Bianca by giving her his secretly-coded "lesson")
Madam, before you touch the instrument,
To learn the order of my fingering,
I must begin with rudiments of art,
To teach you gamut in a briefer sort,

More pleasant, pithy, and effectual
Than hath been taught by any of my trade;
And there it is in writing, fairly drawn.

Hortensio: (Act 3 scene 1, beginning to suspect something might be going on between Cambio and Bianca)
But I have cause to pry into this pedant;
Methinks he looks as though he were in love.
Yet if thy thoughts, Bianca, be so humble
To cast thy wand'ring eyes on every stale,
Seize thee that list: if once I find thee ranging,
Hortensio will be quit with thee by changing.

Kate: (Act 3 scene 2, furious, believing she is being stood up at the altar)
No shame but mine! I must, forsooth, be forced
To give my hand, opposed against my heart,
Unto a mad-brain rudesby, full of spleen,
Who woo'd in haste and means to wed at leisure.
I told you, I, he was a frantic fool,
Hiding his bitter jests in blunt behavior,
And to be noted for a merry man,
He'll woo a thousand, point the day of marriage,
Make friends, invite, and proclaim the banes,
Yet never means to wed where he hath woo'd.

Petruchio: (Act 3 scene 2, explaining why he will marry Kate dressed as he is)
To me she's married, not unto my clothes.
Could I repair what she will wear in me,
As I can change these poor accouterments,
'Twere well for Kate, and better for myself.
But what a fool am I to chat with you,
When I should bid good-morrow to my bride,
And seal the title with a lovely kiss!

Baptista: (Act 3 scene 2, getting on with the wedding feast after Kate and Petruchio have left)
Neighbors and friends, though bride and bride-
  groom wants
For to supply the places at the table,
You know there wants no junkets at the feast.
Lucentio, you shall supply the bridegroom's
  place,
And let Bianca take her sister's room.

Grumio: (Act 4 scene 1, making sure Curtis has prepared everything for Petruchio's return home)
  Why therefore fire, for I have caught extreme cold. Where's the cook, is supper ready, the house trimmed, rushes strewed, cobwebs swept, the serving-men in their new fustian, their white stockings and every officer his wedding garment on? Be the Jacks fair within, the Jills fair without, the carpets laid, and everything in order?

Hortensio: (Act 4 scene 2, agreeing with the disguised Tranio to renounce Bianca's love)

See how they kiss and court! Signior Lucentio,
Here is my hand, and here I firmly vow
Never to woo her more, but do forswear her
As one unworthy all the former favours
That I have fondly flattered her withal.

Tranio: (Act 4 scene 2, explaining the reason for the death sentence on Mantuans who are found in Padua)

'Tis death for anyone in Mantua
To come to Padua. Know you not the cause?
Your ships are stayed at Venice, and the duke,
For private quarrel 'twixt your duke and him,
Hath published and proclaimed it openly.
'Tis marvel, but that you are but newly come,
You might have heard it else proclaimed about.

Kate: (Act 4 scene 3, trying to convince Grumio to bring her food)

The more my wrong, the more his spite appears.
What, did he marry me to famish me?
Beggars that come unto my father's door,
Upon entreaty have a present alms;
If not, elsewhere they meet with charity.
But I, who never knew how to entreat,
Nor never needed that I should entreat,
Am starved for meat, giddy for lack of sleep,
With oaths kept waking, and with brawling fed.
And that which spites me more than all these
  wants,
He does it under name of perfect love
As who should say, if I should sleep or eat,
'Twere deadly sickness or else present death.
I prithee go and get me some repast,
I care not what, so it be wholesome food.

Pedant: (Act 4 scene 4, telling Lucentio that he once stayed at the same hotel as Vincentio)

and, but I be deceived,
Signior Baptista may remember me
Near twenty years ago in Genoa
Where we were lodgers at the Pegasus.

Baptista: (Act 4 scene 4, politely stating the terms that will have to be met before he will allow a marriage between Lucentio and Bianca)

Sir, pardon me in what I have to say;
Your plainness and your shortness please me
  well.
Right true it is, your son Lucentio here
Doth love my daughter and she loveth him,
(Or both dissemble deeply their affections)
And therefore, if you say no more than this—

That like a father you will deal with him,
And pass my daughter a sufficient dower—
The match is made and all is done:
Your son shall have my daughter with consent.

Petruchio: (Act 4 scene 5, telling Vincentio that his son has married Kate's sister and that they are therefore all now related by marriage—note that Petruchio uses the term *father* rather loosely)

Happily met! the happier for thy son.
And now by law, as well as reverent age,
I may entitle thee my loving father—
The sister to my wife, this gentlewoman,
Thy son by this hath married. Wonder not
Nor be not grieved; she is of good esteem,
Her dowry wealthy, and of worthy birth;
Beside, so qualified as may beseem
The spouse of any noble gentleman.

Vincentio: (Act 4 scene 5, not sure whether to believe Petruchio's report of Lucentio's marriage)

But is this true, or is it else your pleasure,
Like pleasant travellers, to break a jest
Upon the company you overtake?

Petruchio: (Act 5 scene 1, arriving at Lucentio's lodging in Padua)

Sir, here's the door, this is Lucentio's house,
My father's bears more toward the market-place;
Thither must I, and here I leave you sir.

Kate: (Act 5 scene 2, telling Bianca and the Widow about wifely duties)

Such duty as the subject owes the prince,
Even such, a woman oweth to her husband.
And when she is froward, peevish, sullen, sour,
And not obedient to his honest will,
What is she but a foul contending rebel
And graceless traitor to her loving lord?

These exercises are designed to help familiarize you with the phrases and words that Shakespeare used and to illustrate how similar they are to our current English language.

The following list contains words and phrases from *The Taming of the Shrew* along with their modern equivalents.

Using these words and phrases:

1. Write a letter from your character in the play to another character and use at least ten of the words or phrases in your letter.
2. Incorporate these words and phrases into your discussions of the play in class.
3. Sneak these words and phrases into conversation when speaking to your family and friends and see how they react. Can you work the phrase into conversation so that they understand you without your having to explain what you mean?

Shakespeare's words	*Modern English*
tell me thy mind	what do you think?
for the time	for now
affected as yourself	feel as you do
put us in readiness	get ready
importune	to urge in a bothersome way
deliver us	save us
froward	disobedient, rebellious
mew	to confine, to shut in
taketh	takes
prefer them hither	send them here
toucheth us both	concerns both of us
think'st thou?	do you think?
pass	to go beyond, exceed
in faith	truly
how say you?	what do you say?
of a sudden	suddenly
counsel me	advise me
canst	can, are able to
marked	noted, observed
'tis	it is
bend thoughts	think up, use your brain
thus is stands	this is how it is
device	plan
content thee	relax, don't sweat it
I have it full	I see it all
in my stead	instead of me
keep his tongue	keep quiet
sith	since
I am content	I'm glad, I'm happy
I pray you	I ask, beg or implore you
descried	discovered
ne'er a whit	not a bit
thyself	you
trow	know
soundly	well
pate	head
compound	resolve, settle
spake	spoke
'twixt	between
come roundly to thee	be frank with you
thou art	you are
peace	be quiet
tarry	wait
hath	has
ta'en	taken
do me grace	do me a favor
well seen	proficient
have leave	have the opportunity
hark you	listen up
whate'er	whatever
woodcock	jerk/dimwit/dodo/birdbrain
lighted on	discovered
to vent	to express
what countryman?	where are you from?
have a stomach	be strong enough
hither	here
beseech	beg, ask, request
readiest	easiest, quickest
attend	wait for
a glass	a mirror
well aimed	good guess
in sooth	in truth, truly
'scape	escape
passing	very, extremely
gamesome	playful
how speed you?	how are you coming along?
in your dumps	depressed
'twixt us twain	between us both
greybeard	old man
struck in years	elderly
outvied	outbid
a cavil	a detail
I am thus resolved	I have decided
'tis in my head	it's my intention
ere	before
take heed	be careful
stays him from	keeps him from
'twere	it were
methinks	I think
over-reach	outsmart
hence	away
entreat	request, invite
prithee	wish, request
look not big	don't be angry
trimmed	neatened
thereby hangs a tale	that reminds me of a story
by this reckoning	by this account

engenders	causes to develop
planteth	instill, engender
hurly	commotion, uproar
resolve me that	inform me of that
wonderful	surprising, marvelous
forsworn	renounced, sworn off
dog-weary	exhausted
an ancient	an old man
credulous	believable
make the matter good	take care of things
spites me	annoys me
repast	food
passing good	very good
how fares	how is
pluck up thy spirits	cheer up
all amort	depressed
apace	quickly
stays your leisure	waits for you
did bespeak	placed an order
doth	does
fit the time	is appropriate or *in fashion*
marred	ruined
sport	play
'longeth	belongs
a tall fellow	a good guy
a weighty cause	an important matter
matched	engaged to be married
it likes me well	it pleases me
hie	hurry
what say'st thou?	what do you say?
tarry	wait
what I list	what I like
but soft	but wait
whither away?	where are you going?
make known	tell, inform
full joyous	very happy
I fly	I'm hurrying, I'm gone
you were best	it would be better if you
what's he?	who is it?
withal	with
flat knavery	downright criminal
lay hands on	arrest
we are undone	all is lost
didst thou	did you
marry sir	truly sir
what concerns it you?	what's it got to do with you?
you mistake	you're wrong
mine	my
hath	has
undone	ruined
wrought	created, made
fear not	don't be afraid
thy	your
is not this well?	isn't this great?
affords	offers

forthwith	immediately
must needs	has to, have to
bid	ask
confer	talk, chat
bodes	means, foretells
laying on	betting on
meet	appropriate

(Note that certain of these words can mean other things, too, but these are their meanings in the context of *Shrew*.)

The rehearsal process

WHO'S WHO AND WHAT'S WHAT IN PUTTING A PLAY TOGETHER

WHO'S WHO

There is first of all the play, then the actors, then the director. The job of the director is to make sure the story gets told. This can entail many elements: working with actors to help them develop their characters, making sure each actor is headed in the right direction, maintaining order in the rehearsal so that work can move along smoothly, assigning people to do props, costumes, etc.

The director is ultimately the benign dictator who makes sure everything comes together at the right time—that's why he or she get the big bucks!

The stage manager is the director's right hand, a combination of sergeant at arms and girl Friday.

Among the stage manager's many jobs are: recording the blocking in a master script, prompting the actors when they forget their lines (that means a stage manager must always be following along in the script during rehearsals), making sure everyone is at rehearsal on time, coordinating the technical elements (props, costumes, etc.), calling break times and gathering everyone together after the break, helping the director maintain an orderly rehearsal. And once the show is in performance, the stage manager must make sure everyone and everything is in the proper place to insure the show will run smoothly and, most importantly, never becoming frazzled!

The stage manager can usually use an assistant or two. Give careful consideration when selecting someone for this position—a good stage manager is invaluable!

CASTING THE PLAY

The first thing we need to do is to *cast* the play, that is, figure out who will play which role. This can be done by having *auditions* for the parts. To do this, people read various scenes from the play, and then the director, teacher, or the other members of the class make determinations of who would be best suited to play a certain role.

Another way to cast is to have the teacher assign roles. Sometimes it is fun to have multiple casts (more than one actor for each part). That way actors can share their ideas in rehearsal and learn from each other.

With multiple casting, the play could then be presented more times in order to give everyone a chance to read or perform. Note too that a single actor might play more than one role. This is known as *doubling*. For example, the actor playing the servant might double as the Pedant or the Widow, depending on the sex of that actor. And Curtis might double as Vincentio. Doubling and double casting will depend on the number of actors available for your production.

Something to keep in mind when casting is that an obvious choice for a role may not always be the best one. Sometimes a *male* part might be better played by a *female* actor or vice versa. Or an actor whose physical characteristics are not exactly what's called for, might actually be able to bring something more interesting to a certain part. So remember to be flexible and open minded in the casting process.

INVESTIGATING THE SCRIPT

Once the casting is determined, it's time to get to work. Professional actors usually begin the rehearsal process by sitting around together and reading the play out loud a number of times. The first time through, we just listen to the story. The next time through, we start discussing the play.

The rules here are usually that anyone may stop and ask a question at any time. It could be a question of the meaning of a word, a discussion of why a character does something, or perhaps a question about where a scene is taking place. In other words, everything and anything that may not be perfectly clear should be examined at this point. This is done to make sure that everyone fully understands what is being said and what is going on in the course of the play.

This can take days or even a week in a professional company (and that's working eight hours a day!). So take your time on this step and be thorough. The more time spent clarifying everything at this stage of the process, the more smoothly the rest of the rehearsal will go.

Once all the questions have been answered, go back and read the play again and note how much richer and clearer the language will be to you.

At this point the decision must be made whether you are going to do a *reading* of the play or a simple production. A reading is a modified performance in which there would be no sets or costumes and is usually done with only the simplest movement. Actors could just be seated in a semicircle facing the listeners, with their scripts in hand, and read the play.

DOING A READING

If you have decided upon a reading, you still must determine how best to tell the story of the play to make it clear and interesting for the audience.

This is done by adding *shape* or *structure* to our work. We do this by going scene-by-scene through the play and (having determined what the scene is about in our previous work) and figuring out how it fits into the overall *arc* of the play, how that scene moves the story forward, and how each character contributes to that movement.

By examining the scenes in this way, we can then determine the *rhythms* that the scene requires for the acting of it: for example, some will need to be fast-paced, some slow, some a combination of both; some will need to be quiet, some raucous; in some, the characters will speak quickly—perhaps overlapping the previous speaker, and in others, the language will be languid or perhaps romantic. All these various elements will add what we refer to as *shape* and *color* to the material.

We do this with each scene and slowly expand our work to include larger sections till the entire shape of the play becomes clear. Experiment, explore and see what works best for your production. The director makes the final decisions because he or she will have the best overview of the play, having been able to watch it all.

The most important element for a reading is a clear understanding of the language, the situation (or story), and the character relationships. These are, after all, the most critical elements of Shakespeare.

This would be an excellent place for most classes to get to. But, for those of you who wish to do a simple staging of the play, read on.

BLOCKING

If you have decided to stage a production of the play, you still must do all the work of shaping discussed in the reading section, only you do this while *blocking* the play.

Blocking is the process of organizing the physical movement of the play. We usually block working one scene at a time and holding our scripts (that is before beginning to memorize our lines.)

We do this because most actors find it much easier to memorize lines when the lines are connected to movements. (Note that the blocking we have offered with the text is merely one way to go, feel free to create movement that feels comfortable for you.)

WORKING SCENES AND MEMORIZING

The next step is to *work scenes* of the play–that is to rehearse them, adjusting the blocking as needed to make sure the actors feel comfortable with the movement and checking that the situations in the text are being properly clarified. It is during this step that we also begin memorizing the lines.

Memorization usually begins to happen on its own at this point, particularly if all the previous discussion work has been thoroughly accomplished. Shakespeare writes so well that his words seem to become the only ones to say in the situations that he has devised. This is not the case with all playwrights!

There are times, though (particularly with longer speeches), when it is necessary to go over and over a section out loud until it is ingrained in the brain and in the muscles of the mouth. (It's amazing how many times on stage, an actor has forgotten a line but his or her mouth still keeps going and knows what to say!) If an actor forgets a line during rehearsal, he or she says the word *line,* and the stage manager (who is following in the script) reads the line to the actor and work goes on.

This period of rehearsal is the longest and most exciting part of the process. As we go over and over each scene, the language and the actions truly become part of us, and we grow to understand a little more about the characters and their situations each time through. During this period it is often said that we are *becoming* the character. In a professional situation, we are lucky if we have four weeks to spend on this part of the process. So again, spend as much time as you can.

Once individual scenes begin to *take shape,* we start putting together larger chunks of the play, perhaps doing three or four scenes in a row and beginning to feel the *flow* of the play and finding the *throughline* of the characters.

Don't forget that this is an ongoing process and that different actors have creative inspirations at different points in the rehearsal period. If someone comes up with a new and exciting idea after blocking has been completed, experiment with it and be willing to change if it turns out to be better. This is the *creative process,* and these are the very instincts and ideas that will make your production unique and wonderful.

RUN-THROUGHS

It is at this point that we put the whole play together and go through it from beginning to end. It is during the run-throughs that we finally get to understand what is needed from us as actors to take our characters from their starting places to where they end up at the end of the play.

TECHS AND DRESSES

Now we add the final elements of props and costumes (sometimes we are lucky enough to have gotten these earlier in our rehearsal process and have been able to incorporate them sooner). But we definitely need everything at this point! These are referred to as the *technical* elements of the production.

Remember, though, that the ultimate element of any Shakespearean production is the incredibly wonderful language through which Shakespeare conveys his ideas. Keep it simple and clear and it will enlighten and uplift...Good show!

Developing a character

AN EXERCISE FOR CREATING A CHARACTER HISTORY

When working on a play, an actor will usually create a *history* or *background* for his or her character. This is the story of the character's life. It is made up by the actor in order to gather insights into the character's psyche and better understand how that character will respond to the various situations that he or she is confronted with in the course of a play.

We create this story by examining the *givens* in the text (that is, the various hints that the playwright has written into or given in the script) and making lists of all the information that we gather.

These include:

1. Everything that is said about the character by other characters in the play.
2. Everything the character says about him- or herself.
3. An examination of the physical characteristics and the physical limitations that the playwright might have specified in the text.

In addition to this information, we get more by asking a series of questions about the character:

1. What does the character want? This is a twofold question:
   a. What does the character want in the big picture of life? Does he or she want to be a movie star? To be rich? To be loved?
   b. What does the character want in each scene? In other words, what is he or she desiring the other characters to do or say?
2. How does the character go about getting those things? Does the character aggressively go after things or is he or she passive? Will she "sell her grandmother"? Is he honest and plodding?
3. How does the character react in various situations with anger? passively? with compassion?
4. How does the character feel about him- or herself?
5. What is his or her environment or social situation? Is this character from a family of fourteen and ignored by everyone? Is he or she from a big city? A small town? A rich family? A well-educated family?
6. How does the character's mind operate? Is he or she quick witted or slow? Plodding or inventive?
7. What is the character's journey through the play? In other words, what is that character like when we first encounter them and when and how does the character evolve, grow, or change during the course of the play? Or does that character remain unchanged?

We find the answers to these questions by scouring the text and by *creating* answers with our imaginations when they are not available. This is precisely why no two actors can ever play a character the same way. Each actor has personally created that character!

We now take the givens we have discovered in the text and combine these with the various answers we have come up with to our series of questions and create from this raw material our character's history.

During rehearsal, we constantly refer back to this history to help us figure out our character's actions and responses to the various situations in the play.

Remember, there are no right or wrong ways to do this. Just be honest in your search and when in doubt, always go back to the text.

Acting techniques, theatrical conventions, and lazzi

For those of you considering doing a performance of the play, here are some basic acting techniques and theatrical conventions to keep in mind.

PACING SHAKESPEARE'S PLAYS

It is generally agreed that in Shakespeare's day, his plays were performed with alacrity. The language moved and the action moved.

With Shakespeare, perhaps more than with any other playwright, there is an acting technique that dictates that as soon as the last line of one scene is spoken, the first line of the next scene comes in hot on its tail.

Language is, after all, the critical element of Shakespeare, and we want all the action to come *on the language*–that is, with the words–unless otherwise specified. This means that when a stage direction says "enter UL X DC" it means that the language begins at the entrance unless otherwise specified. Also, whenever possible, actors should be moving toward their exit with their last lines so that the action and language are continuous.

This does not mean that the actor has to feel rushed or be afraid to take pauses. It's just that for the most part, Shakespeare is best performed without indulgence. As Hamlet says to the players: "Speak the speech I pray you, as I pronounced it to you, *trippingly* on the tongue."

STAGE ETIQUETTE

Another important element for our purposes in performing requires that after exiting from the stage, an actor proceed quietly and unobtrusively around upstage to his or her next entrance and then silently watch the action on stage until it is time to reenter.

Courtesy and cooperation are two of the most important elements in the theater. We work as a team and do all we can to assist our fellow actors and thereby help our production move along smoothly.

MONOLOGUES

If your character has a monologue, you have some choices as to how to deliver it.

Depending on the situation, you could either talk directly to the audience and share your *inner thoughts* with them, or you could do the speech as though you were *thinking out loud* and the audience is overhearing you.

ASIDES

An *aside* is a bit of dialogue that the audience hears, but supposedly the other characters on stage do not hear. Grumio's line in Act 1 scene 2 is an example of this type of aside:

See—to beguile the old folks, how the young folks lay their heads together!

These are usually best executed by having the actor who has the aside say it directly *to the audience* while the other actors go on about their business as though they don't hear it.

Sometimes an aside is directed *to another actor,* such as Tranio's aside to Lucentio in Act 1 scene 1 when he says:

Master! That wench is stark mad, or wonderful froward.

In this case Tranio would direct his aside to Lucentio, and the other actors on stage would continue on as though they had not heard it. This is a theatrical convention that, once established, is easily accepted by an audience.

WHISPERING

A *stage whisper* differs from a real life whisper in that it must be loud enough for the audience to hear it clearly. In the case of the Lucentio and Bianca stage whispering in Act 3 scene 1, Hortensio is probably *straining* to overhear them.

ANGLING OUT

This is a theatrical convention for making sure that the audience can see the actors onstage.

In real life when two people talk to each other, they probably stand face-to-face. On stage it is necessary to stand on an angle facing slightly out to the audience in order to be seen.

When standing on the sides of the stage, it is often necessary for the actor who is nearest the outside to place him or herself a little below and on an angle to the actor who is closer to the center. This is done to make sure the audience can see the action.

This is definitely something to experiment with.

COUNTERING

Countering is adjusting your position on stage to accommodate or balance a movement made by another actor, such as when someone joins a scene already in progress or when an actor is required to cross from one side of you to the other.

We do this to keep adequate spacing between the actors on stage so that the audience can get a clear view of the action.

AD LIBS

When the term *ad lib* is noted in a script, it indicates to the actor that he or she must make up some words or dialogue to *fill the moment.*

In Act 1 scene 1 when Lucentio says, "But stay what company is this?," he is referring to the offstage ad libs which he hears. Hortensio might be heard saying, "Prithee sir, hear me," while Gremio says, "Signior Baptista, neighbor..." then Baptista could say, "No, no gentlemen!" There should be just enough extra dialogue to give Lucentio and Tranio time to *hide* behind the ladder.

Remember that whenever an ad lib is called for, it must be appropriate to the character and to the time in which that character lived!

HIDING BEHIND THE LADDER

The ladder has several functions in this production, one of which is to allow characters to hide behind it in order to observe other scenes unnoticed.

When an actor gets behind it (even partially), he is *hidden* from the other actors onstage. Even when he leans out around it to speak to the audience or to the actor hiding with him, he is still in its protective cocoon. The use of the ladder in this way is an example of a *stage convention.*

Tranio and Lucentio must *establish* it in Act 1 scene 1 when they need a place to hide. After Lucentio says, "But stay; what company is this?," Tranio and Lucentio must take a moment to look at each other, then look around the stage, then, noticing the ladder and both realizing that it's the perfect place, look at each other again, nod, and run behind it. When they lean around it to speak, they do so in the manner of an *aside.*

Once the ladder is established as a hiding place, the audience will accept it as part of the world of the play.

KNOCKING

Stamping on the floor is a *theatrical convention* actors use when there are no actual doors present on a set. If an actor stamps his foot and coordinates it with a knocking motion, the audience will immediately accept this convention. Or the actor might just pretend to knock, and say, "knock, knock, knock," or, if he can make that strangely wonderful *knocking sound* with his tongue, he might do that.

In Act 2 scene 1, it is probably Gremio who *knocks* from offstage since he is the first one to appear onstage. In Act 5 scene 1 when Vincentio is called upon to knock, he shouldn't knock on the ladder itself but stand about a foot away from it and perform the convention.

BOW

An Elizabethan bow is an altogether different animal from a modern one. Elizabethan bows were very courtly and dashing.

Here's the general idea:

Elizabethan *gentlemen* rarely stood with their feet together–but rather with one foot slightly in front of the other and with one hand on their hip–very jauntily.

They stood up tall, head high, eyes looking straight ahead, and tried to appear very sure of themselves (sometimes too sure). Standing around with hunched shoulders, hands in the pockets, looking at the ground was a good way to get shoved aside!

The same proud attitude was maintained while bowing. The bow was a greeting–usually between equals and not a slavish acknowledgment of superiority. (If a bow *was* made to a person of superior rank, the person of lower rank merely bent a little deeper from the waist.)

The mechanics of the bow are:

1. Step back a little with one foot and bend the leg slightly at the knee; keep the front leg straight.
2. As you hold your arms slightly open to the sides, bend forward from the waist–but not too much. Keep the back perfectly straight and the head in line with the back but perhaps at a slight angle.
3. Keep your eyes on the person you are bowing to (unless the person you are bowing to is royalty, they look at the floor!)

Circumstances and relationships will dictate how elaborate or simple a bow should be–so figure out what your character would do in the situation he finds himself in.

SLAPS

In the wooing scene, Kate slaps Petruchio. *Real* slaps onstage take forever to get right and usually involve bruised ear drums and sore jaws–don't do them.

A well-done stage slap is always great to watch and a poor one is always a disappointment. Here is a good way to *fake* a slap–it too will take a lot of practice but with a lot less pain!

Remember that all elements must be agreed upon by the actors involved, rehearsed slowly at first, then increase the speed until it just seems to *happen*.

Kate crosses to Petruchio on the line "That I'll try," plants herself opposite him and looks him in the eye. This serves two purposes: it lets Kate and Petruchio get set and it focuses the audience's attention on their faces. As with magic tricks, getting the audience to focus where you want them to allows the business to work.

Kate then takes her left arm (her downstage arm) back for the *wind up* and brings her hand through aiming for Petruchio's right cheek.

In the meantime, Petruchio is standing with his arms casually at his side. When Kate *slaps* him, Petruchio quickly turns his head upstage at the last moment to avoid the actual contact and, as he does this, he slaps his right hand against his left to produce the slapping sound.

Once the *timing* of this bit is established for both actors, it must be adhered to steadfastly–no surprises for your fellow actors, only for the audience!

SLOSHED/DRUNK

Acting drunk onstage is a delicate matter. Actors often go so far overboard that it becomes totally unbelievable. The basics of drunkedness are: slurred speech, the inability to stand up straight, blurred vision, slowing of response time, and often the good old hiccup.

The way to achieve this is to *play against* the alcohol. That means that the actor must try hard *not* to appear drunk. So while his speech is slurred, he is trying very hard to enunciate clearly. It is this overenunciation that makes him appear to be slurring.

The sober person has no trouble standing up straight because his *center* is running straight up and down from head to foot. But a drunk's center keeps shifting so that his body is constantly struggling to keep in alignment. This is why a drunk appears to be swaying.

As with the other elements, he must work hard to *focus* and even to keep his eyes open. Also an occasional well-timed hiccup escaping his effort to conceal them can be very effective.

An excellent way to learn drunk technique is to watch a good actor playing drunk on T.V. or film and analyze his or her actions and then copy them. Copying or stealing from other actors is a time honored tradition in the theater. It is one of the ways we pass on the techniques of acting from one generation of actors to the next.

LAZZI

Lazzi is the Italian term for what we generally refer to as comic bits, business, schtick, or gags. We will give some specific examples of lazzi that you may wish to use in *Shrew*, or you may choose to make up your own.

You can find other examples of lazzi by watching any of the great physical comedians past or present and stealing from them. (Note that stealing in the theater is meant as a great form of flattery. Just remember never to steal a bit from someone else in your show–that's theirs for the time being!)

The nose-flicking lazzi which Kate pulls on Hortensio in Act 1 scene 1 is your standard "Three Stooges" bit–though who knows where they got it from. What follows is some specifically choreographed lazzi for particular moments in the play.

Stool Lazzi

The idea of this lazzi, and indeed all moments on stage, is to make them seem as if they just happened, flawlessly and effortlessly. If the audience ever gets ahead of you (sees it coming), all is lost. To insure that a lazzi works, take your time and work slowly and repeatedly until it can be performed with seeming ease.

For this lazzi, you'll need two short stools (standard chair height) that are light in weight. Petruchio must set these stools during his monologue in Act 2 scene 1 so that they will be in position for the lazzi.

This means that he must position them so that he can sit across them with ease and so that Kate will have them in the proper position for her kick. The two actors will have to work out the details of this according to their own physical requirements, and Petruchio must rigidly adhere to whatever has been determined as he places the stools.

The idea of this bit is that Kate becomes so angry and frustrated during the duel of wits that she resorts to violence and in the process of trying to hurt Petruchio, she injures herself.

Here is how it works:

Petruchio has seated Kate on the stage left stool as he is speaking his "No not a whit" speech. When he reaches the word "gamesome," Kate jumps up and stands slightly up left of the stool–she's not about to sit if that's what Petruchio wants her to do.

When she rises, Petruchio sits down on the stool on the word "courteous" as though to imply that Kate has just graciously offered him the stool. This makes Kate even madder–so mad that on the word "affable," she tries to kick the stool out from under Petruchio. She hopes that he will land on the floor but, instead, only succeeds in hurting her own foot.

Here's how to do it: Petruchio sits on the stage left stool and places his right hand on the stage right stool, he crosses his left leg over his right leg and then raises himself very slightly off the stage left stool–imperceptibly so only he knows that he is supporting his weight with his legs and his right arm–so that when Kate kicks the stool, it scoots out from under him. This leaves Petruchio sitting on nothing and looking very cool.

Petruchio then looks at the stool, which should land about three feet in front of him, then at Kate, then back at the stool, then out to the audience and says his next line. Trust us, it works!

In the meantime Kate, who has positioned herself up left of the stool, hauls off and kicks the stool with her right foot hard enough to make it shoot forward about three feet (doing this with such control that the actress never actually hurts her foot–practice with various stool positions to determine how this will work best).

After the kick, Kate grabs her right foot as though in great pain and hops up and down on her left foot getting herself into position down-left-center for the rope lazzi as she continues with her lines.

Rope Lazzi

Petruchio now realizes that he must bring the discussion to an end, and he seizes his chance while Kate is somewhat incapacitated dealing with her foot.

He takes out the rope (which he has prepared during his monologue by adjusting the size of the loop and arranging it so that it can be easily handled) and places the loop over the hopping Kate's head, bringing it down to about elbow level, and cinches it up. The amazed Kate just stands there, arms at her sides.

Petruchio then reaches up to Kate's left shoulder and starts her spinning counterclockwise. Kate will make two complete turns as Petruchio walks clockwise around her ending up on Kate's right while winding the rope lower and lower around Kate until it ends up around Kate's wrists. Petruchio now loops the end of the rope under one of the circles of rope around Kate and pulls it through to secure it.

Note that whenever two actors are doing a bit together, everything must be timed so that they are in total control of their own movements. This means that when Petruchio *spins* Kate, it only *appears* as though he is controlling the action. Kate must actually be in control of her own movements at all times so that she never loses her balance.

Petruchio now has Kate on a leash and can lead her around, and she is constricted so that she must hop along behind. This will probably take several hours of rehearsal to perfect, so take your time and be patient.

Try and time the dialogue so that Petruchio has tied Kate up by the time he says, "I will marry you." At this point Kate opens her mouth wide to protest, and at that moment Petruchio stuffs his *handkerchief in her mouth* to keep her quiet. Kate can now only hop and make muffled noises of protest. (Note that here, as with all business, extreme care must be taken to rehearse this bit so that Kate is in no danger of being hurt. It must be timed so that she can be ready to bite down on the handkerchief so that she is actually holding it in her teeth.)

None of the above is written in stone. Modify or replace with something else if you prefer—whatever works best for your production.

In general comedy should be played briskly, with verve and quickness but never with the sense of being rushed. Pauses and slow passages will then serve as contrasts, set-ups, and payoffs to the main thrust of the action.

Remember too that comedy only *looks* easy. A lot of careful work went into creating that *illusion*. Be patient and diligent in your attention to detail and, most importantly, have fun!

Prayer lazzi

For this bit, Petruchio says his line, "Will you give thanks, sweet Kate, or else shall I?" then, not waiting for an answer, he bows his head, puts his hands together in prayer, and quickly says "Anno domino, dominee, Asata dunca dave."

This is Petruchio's version of a gibberish Latin prayer. It should be played briskly and not be dwelt upon. It's merely another little bit of Petruchio's joyous insanity.

After the prayer, Petruchio looks up, sees the meat, and goes on with his lines.

"Here's a marvelous convenient place for our rehearsal"

A SUGGESTED SET

For our purposes, a simple set that serves for all locales is best. We suggest a bare space. Masking tape on the floor can delineate the entrances and exits. When an actor crosses that line, he or she has *entered* or *exited* the stage.

The only *set pieces* needed are three short stools and a ladder which is about six feet high. The ladder will have *signs* displayed on it to indicate where a scene is taking place (see prop notes).

With this and all other technical elements, simplicity is the key factor; with Shakespeare, language is foremost! See page 146 for a set design.

"We will have rings and things and fine array"

SUGGESTIONS FOR COSTUMES AND PROPS

For our purposes, props and costumes should be kept to an absolute minimum. This will not only make it easier to produce the play, but it will keep our focus firmly on the language, where it needs to be.

Costumes

Think about how your character might dress if he or she were around today and find something appropriate from what you have easily available to you (the actors playing older characters might check out their parents' closets). Here are some suggestions:

KATE—a long-sleeved turtleneck and a long skirt or jeans (she is a rebel); add a gauzy piece of fabric for her wedding veil and a few flowers for a bouquet; her cap may either be the one the tailor brought or whatever cap the actress has available. When she arrives at Petruchio's house, she has put some mud on her hands and face, mussed up her hair, and half-untucked her shirt to indicate the wear and tear of the trip (Petruchio and Grumio should do similar type things).

PETRUCHIO—a long-sleeved turtleneck, jeans, boots, some sort of short jacket (perhaps a jean jacket or a bomber, whatever you have readily available). For the wedding scene, Petruchio is described as wearing an old jacket, old pants, and two different boots (or shoes), he is being outrageous—create a bizarre combination of clothes for yourself. He can change back to his original costume during Act 4 scene 2 if he likes.

LUCENTIO—long-sleeved turtleneck, jeans, a brimmed hat, and a suit jacket or blazer. He will give Tranio the jacket and hat when they exchange clothes.

TRANIO—a t-shirt and jeans, a baseball cap. He will give Lucentio his cap when they swap clothes.

BIONDELLO and GRUMIO—t-shirts and jeans, caps if they choose. Grumio can change into a pair of shorts and cowboy boots for the wedding scene or something equally outrageous.

BAPTISTA, GREMIO, VINCENTIO and the PEDANT—they could all be wearing dark-colored, long-sleeved, button down the front type shirts, perhaps even with ties, and slacks (or suits or blazers if available—they are your grown-up business types).

CURTIS and SERVANT—sweatshirts, sweatpants, and sneakers.

HORTENSIO—brightly colored shirt unbuttoned at the neck (maybe even a gold-chain) and slacks—he thinks he's a real dude.

BIANCA—short skirt and blouse.

WIDOW—long skirt and blouse.

TAILOR—pretty spiffily dressed, even elegant, perhaps a suit or slacks and nice shirt.

Props

LADDER—The ladder should be your basic step-ladder type, about six feet tall. The first position for it is in the UR area of the stage, about three feet in from the upstage and stage right limits of the set. It is set so that the steps of the ladder are facing stage left and the "A" side is toward the audience.

SCENE SIGNS—this *theatrical convention* of noting where a scene takes place using *signs* can be accomplished with a roll of paper towels, a magic marker, and some clothesline rope, Using a roll of plain white paper towels and the magic marker, print the locations of the scenes—one per sheet—on the first ten sheets, then roll the sheets back onto the roll so that the sheets read as follows (extra credit for lettering in Elizabethan style!):

"Town Square"
"Hortensio's House"
"Baptista's House"
"Town Square"
"Petruchio's House"
"Town Square"
"Petruchio's House"
"Town Square"
"On the Road"
"Lucentio's House"

Run a five-foot piece of rope through the paper towel roll, tie one end of the rope around one leg of the ladder about four feet up the ladder just above a rung (so it will stay in place), and then tie the rope off at the same height on the other leg of the ladder, positioning the paper towels so that the sheets roll off downstage and can be easily unrolled and torn off as required in the play.

STOOLS—chair height, light-weight, wooden or perhaps those molded plastic garden tables from your backyards.

CAMBIO and LUCENTIO'S DISGUISES—toy store-type plastic glasses with nose and mustache attached; they should be identical.

BOOKS FOR CAMBIO—in Act 1 scene 2, Cambio comes on carrying two or three hardcover books.

ROPE—clothesline type, about eighteen feet long, with a slip knot tied at one end to tie Bianca's hands and later for Petruchio to put around Kate.

HANDKERCHIEF—any kind, make sure it's clean!

LUTE—a guitar, banjo, mandolin, ukulele, whatever you have (toy or real).

PACKET OF BOOKS—two smallish, hardcover books that Bianca and Lucentio will use later in Act 4 scene 2.

GAMUT FOR HORTENSIO—rolled up piece of paper.

LATIN BOOK FOR LUCENTIO—any hardcover books.

SWORDS FOR PETRUCHIO and GRUMIO—plastic toy sword, *pirate* type perhaps, or pieces of wood with crosspiece attached as a "hilt" to keep it from falling out of your belt (Grumio's should be shorter than Petruchio's if possible).

BOWL OF WATER—any small plastic or wooden bowl filled with confetti which will be the "water" poured on Kate.

TRAY OF FOOD FOR GRUMIO—unbreakable tray with unbreakable plates and cups, plastic or papier mâché food.

PENCIL FOR LUCENTIO—sharp-pointed regular pencil to impale the flower for Bianca in Act 4 scene 2.

PLATE OF MEAT FOR PETRUCHIO—plate with plastic or papier mâché food (Kate will then act like she's eating).

BOOK FOR PEDANT—any hardcover book.

CAP AND GOWN FOR TAILOR—a long dress with long sleeves and a small hat (check your parents' closet again).

Glossary

THEATRICAL CONVENTION

An agreed upon action (that may or may not be used in everyday life) which we *establish* on stage to convey something unusual that the script may require–for example, using the paper towel signs to *set each scene* is a theatrical convention.

ESTABLISH

To *establish* is to set up a theatrical convention such as when Grumio tears off the "Town Square" to reveal the "Hortensio House" sign. He has now established that we are using these signs to indicate the various locations in Padua.

THEATRICAL LICENSE

Liberties we take with the script to achieve certain results that we as actors, directors, or editors are going for.

BLOCKING

The organized physical movement of a play.

REHEARSAL PROCESS

The time between the casting of a play and the opening.

READING

An organized, rehearsed presentation of a play in which the actors read from the script rather than memorizing the lines. (Could be done seated or with simple movements.)

SHAPE

A clear definable beginning, middle, and end to a scene or to the entire play. (Also referred to as *arc*.)

THROUGHLINE

This usually refers to the series of actions a character performs throughout the course of a play in quest of his desires.

CUT

In theatrical terms, to *cut* is to eliminate from the script.

VERNACULAR

Vernacular is defined by Webster's as "using a language or dialect native to a region or country rather than a literary, cultured, or foreign language." For our purposes, then, vernacular would be our everyday American English.

DOUBLING

When one actor plays two parts, this is referred to as *doubling*. For example, the actor playing Curtis might alter his appearance and return as Vincentio.

STAGE

The designated area where the action of a play takes place.

ENTER

To walk into the area referred to as the stage.

EXIT

To leave the stage area.

CROSS (often abbreviated "X")

To move across the stage to the area indicated by whatever stage direction follows the term (xing then means–*crossing* in the stage directions).

STAGE TERMINOLOGY

Note that the following stage terminology is indicated from the point of view of the actor, onstage, looking out to the audience.

SR (stage right): Toward the right side of the stage as viewed by the actor when facing an audience.

SL (stage left): Toward the left side of the stage from the actor's point of view.

US (up stage): Towards the rear of the stage.

DS (down stage) Toward the front of the stage.

C (center): The center of the stage.

We combine these terms to describe all the various sections of the stage. For example:

UR (up right): The upper part of the stage on the right side.

DL (down left): The lower part of the stage on the left side.

DRC (down right center): The lower part of the stage to the right of center stage.

DLC (down left center): The lower part of the stage to the left of center stage.

Use the chart on page 145 to determine other designations. These designations are only approximate. If you are using the suggested stage directions, don't feel you have to stand dead center in the DRC circle if that is indicated–do whatever looks and feels best for your space and your production.

Additional projects

1. Write out the story of what happens to your character during the course of the play when he or she is not onstage–where are they and what are they doing?

2. Go to the library and look in art books at pictures of the sixteenth century. Observe how the people of Shakespeare's time dressed and stood and carried themselves. Observe their surroundings, their homes and their facial expressions. (If you're lucky enough to live in a city with a museum–check it out.)

3. Look on a map of Italy and locate the various cities that are mentioned in *Shrew*. Note certain discrepancies in Shakespeare's geography: A *sailmaker* from Bergamo? Where's the water?

4. Do an improvisation of what might have happened when Cambio and Licio first go in to meet Kate and Bianca. How does Hortensio end up with Kate and what are Bianca and Lucentio doing?

5. Act out the scene that takes place when Tranio takes Baptista and the Pedant to sign the marriage agreement.

6. Find other situations like these that are *referred* to in the play but not actually part of the action and make up an improvisation around them.

7. Observe people you come in contact with and notice their traits and idiosyncrasies. Look for things that you might be able to use to develop aspects of your character in *Shrew*. For example, is there a girl who's extremely self-centered or coy whose qualities might be used by the actress playing Bianca? Watch these people and then try to incorporate these aspects of their personality into your character.

8. Write out a list of adjectives that best describes the various aspects of your character.

9. Draw a diagram of Padua, locating the places mentioned in *Shrew*—the town square, Baptista's house, Hortensio's house, the church, etc. Determine how they are all related to each other.

10. Write a love letter from your character to the object of your desire—in character.

You get the gist. Come up with a research project that interests you and pursue it. The more we know about a play and its elements, the better we understand and enjoy it.

Bibliography

Comic Transformations in Shakespeare
Ruth Nevo
Methuen and Co., Ltd. 1980

The New Cambridge Shakespeare:
The Taming of the Shrew
Ed. Ann Thompson
Cambridge University Press 1984

The Taming of the Shrew:
A Comparative Study of Oral and Literary Versions
Jan Harold Brunvand
Garland Publishing, Inc. 1991

The Bankside Shakespeare:
The Taming of the Shrew
Appleton Morgan, ed.
The Shakespeare Society of New York 1888

Shakespeare's Sexual Comedy
Hugh M. Richmond
The Bobbs-Merrill Company, Inc. 1971

Shakespeare and the Traditions of Comedy
Leo Salinger
Cambridge University Press 1974

The Love Story in Shakespearean Comedy
Anthony J. Lewis
University Press of Kentucky 1992

Courtship In Shakespeare
William G. Meader
King's Crown Press 1952

Shakespeare's Comedies
Robert Ornstein
University of Delaware Press 1986

The Woman's Part:
Feminist Criticism of Shakespeare
Lenz, Greene, and Neely, eds.
University of Illinois Press 1980

Friends and Lovers:
The Phenomenology of Desire in Shakespearean Comedy
W. Thomas MacCary
Columbia University Press 1985

Wooing, Wedding, and Power:
Women in Shakespeare's Plays
Irene G. Dash
Columbia University Press 1981

The Taming of the Shrew
H.J. Oliver, ed.
Clarendon Press 1982

The Commedia dell'Arte
Giacomo Oreglia, trans. Lovett F. Edwards
Hill and Wang 1968

Commedia dell'Arte:
An Actor's Handbook
John Rudlin
Routledge 1994

Making a Match:
Courtship in Shakespeare and his Society
Ann Jennalie Cook
Princeton University Press 1991

The Taming of the Shrew
Sir Arthur Quiller-Couch and John Dover Wilson, eds.
The Syndics of the Cambridge University Press
1928

Shakespearean Comedy
Maurice Charney, ed.
New York Literary Forum 1980

The Story of English
McCrum, Cran, and MacNeil
Viking Press 1986

The Plays of Shakespeare
Howard Staunton, ed.
G. Routledge 1858–1861

Shakespeare Lexicon and Quotation Dictionary
Alexander Schmidt, revised Gregor Sarrazin
Dover Publications Inc. 1971

Asimov's Guide to Shakespeare
Isaac Asimov
Avenel Books 1978

Stage Terminology

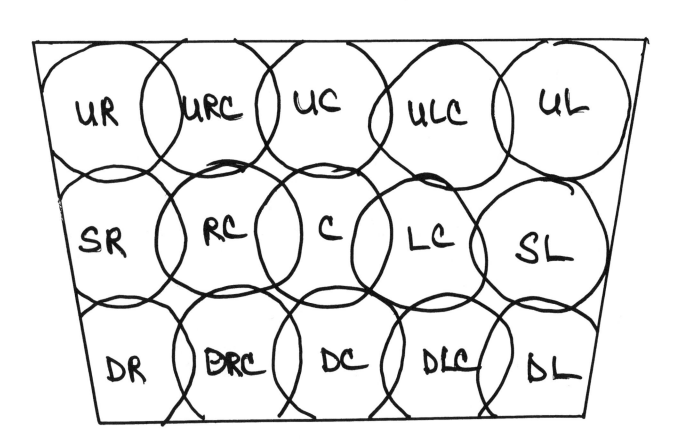

Set Design

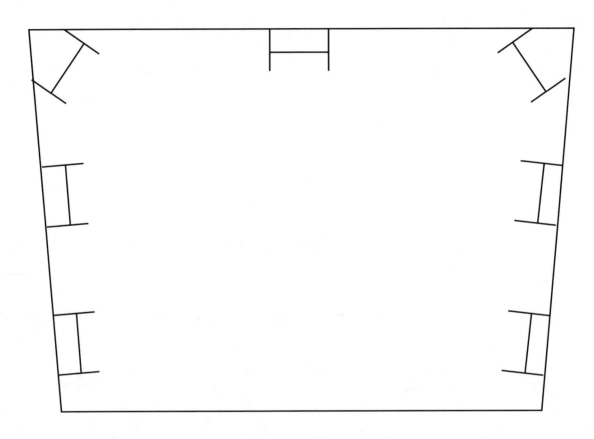

indicates entrance/exit